Hazel

with love
thank for
your belief.

[illegible]

5/10/02

~~07~~ da_imej@hotmail.com

Emotional Condensation

ISBN 0-9542492-0-8

Published by Da Imej
P.O. Box 37337, London, N1 7XU

Cover photo by Abi Akinniyi @ index photography

Typeset and Layout by George Sabapathy @ sponge

Printed by
DPS
77 Gt Titchfield Street
London, W1W 6RN

Emotional Condensation

Junior Ola Dimeji

PROPS TO. . .

GOD. MY MAKER, MY HEAVENLY FATHER, HE WHO BLESSES ME, HE WHO REPLENISHES ME, HE WHO SUSTAINS ME, HE WHO GIVES ME REWARDS ME. I THANK YOU.

My daughters Louise and Jasmine. I love you. I thank God for your existence. I thank you for your patience.. Though things aint ideal, as God would have them be.You know no one loves you like me. ,

Daddy.

My Mother. I know you rest in peace with God in Heaven. Thank you for your strength and selfless love.. Your spirit lives on in me and your grandchildren.

My Father Ola Dimeji. . . Well I am part you. We will play chess again soon.

My Sister Shade, and my nephews (Marcus), Mathias, Miciah, Mishael.

My Brother Jimi. Thanks for being the artistic inspiration early on till I came my into my own. Thanks for allowing God into your life, I don't need to worry about you.

My Brother K. Sup? Thanks for enduring check out the big book Romans 5'3".Perservere my brother. Perservere.I love you.

My adopted fams Coker and Swarey-Cole thank you for your support and love. The family friends that honour my mothers memory and every one that believe in me. I thank you.

Dayo Sowunmi. Goose. My co-pilot, my wingman, my navigator, wherever. Naija, here or Down Under with me forever. Luv ya.

DA and Wale.. All the way from Naija to Philly to Californ . I . A. luv ya.

Mr R. Taiwo, My Ambassador of quarn. (Whatever that is) for your pragmatic balance to the emotional. Thanks.

Skin and Funmi. Your appreciation and love from back in the day till now. Love back atcha

The rest of the Airforce squadron and friends from Naija.Couger, Viper, Rapon and Jide Bada. The gals from Motown Charlie, Xplore. . .Further back in the day. 3B, Patrick and Tayo. Luv ya

Adele, Christine, Lili , my sisters. For your advice, appreciation and friendship. Joy a friend in a Millenium it's our hat thing. Vicky in Maryland thanks for your belief and hospitality stay strong. J'Omigie Nation, how much for the negatives? Monica you are special. Mmmmm, I thought you were.. Heather, I'll call you after seven. . .

Hills, GT, Chuckii, Simon, El Crisis, Brother Courtney, Allon, Phenzwaan, Samantha, Remi, Kourtney Harper and Vannessa. For your creative spirit and drive. I thank you.

The Pampering Club for their endorsment, their vision, providing a forum. I love you. All the events that I have performed at, thanks to the respective organisers. Special shout out to Mr Cee.

Those I met on my gap year. Oct 91 to July 92. My Peeps at Brent Park.Sept 93 to Aug 99. Dollars Man! Dream Team, Finchley N12, Jul 94 to Aug 97. My Niggas on the Night Crew! White and Black, all of y'all Sept 97 to Feb 99. The Fine Young Cannon Balls Oct 99 to Dec 00. And still counting. . .

Couples Junior and Jess, Michael and Marcia, Richard and Pauline, Bunmi and Bukky, Albert and Remi. Something to believe in.

And finally, wether or not this is a lady I've allready met or mentioned as an individual, or in a collective.

To my Soul Mate.

GUEST LIST

Forward

Da Imej

A man's work is never done. A creative soul never rests; it battles for form in an ever-changing world. The only way to trace the outline of transitional conception is to look at the image it casts. All this was clear to me the first time I heard Junior Ola Dimeji reading. I couldn't decide if it was Shakespeare's ghost, or the spirit of hip-hop speaking through him. The poetic inventiveness was evident, but his lyrical stylings had a beat in them that "Big Will" never danced to. I stopped trying to classify him and just listened to Da Imej.

For the reasons, I have stated above, I considered it a worthwhile challenge to edit Junior's work. Indeed I knew that all I could really do was to help translate work created as dialogue into the monologue of written words.

Junior's work covers issues of race, manhood, love and self-fulfilment with a witty slant that is uniquely his. His influences are diverse. He employs repetition in the fashion of ancient African praise songs but writes in the syntax of cosmopolitan streets from Lagos through New York to London.

To read this collection is to journey through the mind of a black man who, in is his own words, "calls a spade a spade"! You need to unzip your prejudices and drop your preconceptions. You have to come to it naked. Can you handle it?

Nii Parkes, Author of "Eyes of a Boy, Lips of a Man."

Emotional Condensation

My Name Is

My name is, what? My name is, what? My name is, what? Ola Dimeji.
Nah I ain't slim shady!
That bleached blond Wigger, the wanna be Nigger
I'm African, specifically Nigerian and of my heritage, I couldn't be prouder.
See I'm down for my people endorse and accept my culture
But for doing so, sometimes I'm told I got a chip on my shoulder.
Now how does that figure?
When my peeps bailed hay for no pay back in the day
For some 400 years maybe longer
But I ain't going there cos they say
What don't kill ya makes you stronger.

I'm proud of my identity
My name is, what? My name is, what? My name is, what? Ola Dimeji
Come on say it right, Cos the letters are English and the phonetics are simple
But you still can't get your head around a few Yoruba syllables
Typical ignorant apathy, got no love for an ex colony
What was that go back to my country
I might just do that someday, can I take the crown jewels with me?
No way? OK I'll just hustle here cos I'm an economic refugee.

And please no frontin' with that patronising grin
I know you ain't feelin it I know it ain't from within
How? You see there's a certain sensitivity that comes with my dark brown skin
It's standard issue, known as melanin, and the patent ain't pending.
So turn off that Simply Red, Tim Westwood, Ali G shit, this right here is the real thing
Check the profile,
No fake smile,
Thick lips,
Afro wearing,
Shorts drinking,
Pepper eating,
Circumcised dick having
Straight up, African Black Male!

My name is, what? My name is, what? My name is, what? Ola Dimeji
You heard me.
So say it right like I told ya, 'bout chip on my shoulder.

MY NAME IS ______________________________

Emotional Condensation

Ladies and Gentlemen, Brothers and Sisters,
Are you gathered here today to experience to witness, the art the business
Of poetry and other spoken forms of self expression?
This mode of social observation, recognition of self and collective identification,
Enlightening insight and sober reflection on various topics,
Relationships, where boy meets girl, girl meets boy.
Scenarios and revelations of intro and retrospective thoughts and emotions
A psycho analysis of a world in crisis, you may or may not agree with all this,
But it's just my way of thinking, my brand of self expression
A net result of my thought collection
Using poetry as a vector, rewind selector. I said using poetry as a vector.
But does that make me a poet? No it,
Doesn't. This is just emotional condensation.

When you close your eyes to conceptualise, da imej of a poet, what is it?
Some higher plain reaching, spiritual teaching, revolution preaching
Ankh wearing, soul bearing, prophetic, Afro centric,
Daily meditating, establishment berating, incense burning,
Haiku writing, sonnet reciting, higher or hieroglyphic learning
Shakespearean, authoritarian, guru, mister or sister?
Well these aren't attributes that I necessarily display
And I ain't ever been to Egypt, or for that matter on any package holiday.
My poetry is just self expression, a facet, an extension
It is essentially emotional condensation.

It's honest and diverse. I ain't trying to coerce, OK I do sometimes
In my writing, speaking straight up, or in my rhymes
Bringing you round to my way of thinking.
Without imposing, a little assertive, sometimes subjective, hopefully impressive,
Use of diction. And at this juncture I pause to stress, to mention
This is my perspective, my opinion. It ain't about competition.
The interpretation of my thoughts using words for mediation
I could spark a revelation. Bring you out of the dark, into illumination
With a little emotional condensation

Representation? Are you more brown and down cos you got a big head wrap?
Cos you dress hip-hop or hug on a handshake? I think that's crap.
It ain't just my imagination, but my observation is some people,
Black folk not Caucasian go on like they're straight from some Nubian nation
And even though I've distinguished that I am specifically, Yoruba, Nigerian
They're still ignorant enough to ask, "Do you speak African?"
Inevitably it leads to my irritation,
But the laws of society demand that I limit my frustration
Otherwise by now I'd be doing time, with no option of probation.
If we are all being honest and real we are all on a level par.
This is just a little something from the repertoire, of da imej.
Thank you for your attention, There endeth my emotional condensation.

EMOTIONAL CONDENSATION

No Comparison

Prologue

The word like, L.I.K.E. is frequently used in rap poetry and spoken word
On forums such as those that I have been to and at this that I am about to be heard
So I challenged myself to be the one prove it could be done,
A piece with the L word in short supply
Do we sometimes trivialise, over-simplify, as we try to paint a picture in the minds eye
Of certain scenarios feelings or situations
Do we use metaphors or make comparisons, that don't necessarily do justice
Should we leave them be for what they are or what it is, what it is, what it is
Well there's nothing like this.

Monologue

Fulfiling your true purpose in this life
When a man asks a woman, will you be my wife?
Signing on and third world famine and strife... No comparison

Being incarcerated as an innocent man
Driving again after a two year and six month ban
Black skin, a fake tan... No comparison

Having your mother die in your arms
Holding your first child in the same arms
Responsibility of a parent protecting that child from harm... No comparison

Simultaneous orgasms, uh huh the uni-cum
Having your heart broke by your girl when you swore she was the one
Dairylea with Hovis, cheese and bun. No comparison

My monologue continues,
Still wary of the words I choose,
I reiterate my intent to use the L word sparingly.
Speaking in rhymes not riddles so that you get me.
Breaking it down keeping it tight
Not scattered so that you can gather it
I'm in effect mode, on a roll, mid flow
Taking it slow but no you can't stop it.
It's so heavy, I had to drop it, yet light enough for you to lift it.
It will add up so you can figure it.
Yeah I'm branching out but you can still twig it.
And it ain't too deep, so can you dig it?

This piece began in my mind, from thoughts that I had
Scribbled on a piece of paper but my hand writing's bad
So I transferred my thoughts on to digital format with my IBM ThinkPad
Now it's memorised here in my mind, yeah I can say it blind
And I will use the word like just six times
Once for each of the degrees of separation that distinguish Da Imej
The man you see, the man you may or may not like
That is the fifth time, as I conclude this rhyme
Delivered to a kickin' crowd with this here mike
Satin smooth, Latin for which had to be proved is
Quad erat demonstrandum
Da Imej, No comparison ain't nothin' like this

NO COMPARISON

Can I Get an Overdraft?

It's the last day of the month. That means payday to me
But boy I don't know how I've been lasting
This month's gone on and on, was it forty days long?
I'm so hungry it's like I've been fasting.
Even before I see my pay, the rent has gone for my flat
But I'm OK with that, cos its shelter for my head and it's bigger than my hat.
How about the rest of my money?
Well I put aside a hundred to take out my honey
Actually it was a hundred and fifty,
See the girl's good for me and I didn't wanna make the Sista vex,
Besides, her birthday gets here before my next pay cheque.

How about my direct debits? Well I'm a have to give the Council Tax a miss.
That's about £50.00 saved to help me through this.
I never called the Police, the ambulance or the Fire Brigade
Cos the Met don't work they just get paid
And do they really give a damn 'bout an IC3 like me anyway?
I got my landline on receiving only, so my boys still call me.
My mobile got text and free weekends so I still keep in touch with my friends.

It's serious no joke, I couldn't even afford to check out this new club
Yeah I admit I'm broke. But don't you dare call me a scrub
So what if I ain't got a car, times are hard!
I get around; you see I got my travel card
Anyway my girl got a ride and she loves me for what's inside.
She' got my back, keeps it real and my focus on the right path
But I'm gonna have to ask my bank still . . .
Can I get an overdraft?

CAN I GET AN OVERDRAFT?

Soul Mate

I don't even know if I've meet you yet,
Or if you've been watching me, but I don't wanna let
You slip by unnoticed, like an opportunity missed
Unaware of what we are meant to share
Soul Mate, are you out there?
See, I've gone as far as I can alone.
So I' been hopin' for a certain someone
You know, smart graceful and strong
Preferably with a darker brown skin tone
To love and nurture as my very own.
I need a black woman to reciprocate, can you relate?
I'm that familiar stranger, your Soul Mate.

Doin' domestics' ain't nuthin but a thing!
I hand wash my own draws and shirts.
I can even iron pleated skirts!
And I will ease every hurt that you ever had.
From when you was a baby teething bad,
First knee graze in the playground
Period pains to your last broken heart, I'll be around
To erase all of that.
We can argue fight disagree and debate
Make up again and again and then. Make love till it's late.
Have I seen you, or you seen me and thought "déjà vu"?
Talk to me Soul Mate, I'm calling you.

Where were you in the latter part of the 20th century?
Were you breaking boys' hearts in the eighties?
Find yourself in the nineties? Or find yourself misinvestin'
Emotion devotion and time like me?
Did you get back when you gave
Were you true did you behave?
Cos I wear my heart on my sleeve does that mean sucker on my forehead
Cos I admit, a few times I've been misled.
Mistaken those womanly wiles for genuine affection
But I'm cool now a better man for another harsh lesson
Can I be the man I am with you on a clean slate?
If so, is the woman you are, or wanna be, my Soul Mate?

Do We Share This Dream?

Here I lie awake again, the same as every night
Wondering, were we meant to be?
Afraid to close my eyes and torture my mind
With the visions of you that I always see
How I wish we had fell in stride
And all those feelings I kept inside
Thinking of you and what might have been
I'd like to know, do we share this dream?

Do you wish to go back through time?
And change all your wrongs?
Or form fantasies of you and me,
Knowing that I'm gone?
What went wrong? I can only guess
We were in awe of feelings that we didn't express
It could have been an ocean, it was only a stream.
Is it only my mind, or do we share this dream?

Cos we were just friends and nothing more
Given a chance but we didn't score
But if you curse your pride for all its cost
Now that I'm gone forever lost
Then if so, you are not alone
Cos I sure regret the chance I've blown
To live what now is just a fantasy
That I wonder if you share with me.

Here I lie awake again, the same as every night
Wishing that I had foreseen,
That you and I wouldn't make it, I wish we did and wonder
Do we share this dream?

DO WE SHARE THIS DREAM

I Cant Help It

It's like an involuntary action, an impulsive disorder
Sometimes I think Ioughtta, stop, but I'm doing it without thinking.
While I'm thinking of you, I'm in a daze, eyes glazed and staring without blinking.
Going days . . .a'ight hours without eating or drinking.
To say I got it bad . . .
I got to pray about it. Wish I had control over it
But I like the feeling of being with you. Could I live without it?
Friends say its love. I don't beg to differ or doubt it.
If it is, I'm ready to declare and shout it.
But should I?

Hold back. Cos guys' ain't supposed to be this emotional, right?
Maybe I should front, be more rational, but if I do I might
Confuse you like I'm confused. I don't know what to do.
I' been reading bout men being from Mars and women from Venus
To try and figure out, what it is about us.
To try and understand what I'm going through.
My minds on you even when I. . .
And it ain't like I choose to.
You're on my mind like homepage, by default.
It ain't my fault but it feels so good. So I wouldn't help it even if I could.
I can't help it.

I CAN'T HELP IT

I Wanna Know You

I wanna know you. Like Bill Clinton knows how to lie, like a bird knows how to fly.
I wanna know your story, will you talk with me, walk with me. Tell it to me.
Good or bad, happy or sad. Let's get together. Damn it, let's stay together.
We could sit of at the dock of the bay or stay up on the roof.
Are you frontin' playin aloof? Or you thinkin' I've been drinkin something 60% proof?
I'm sober, like I told ya just wanna get to know ya.
Are ya just Cruisin like Smokie, or just a plain Drifter?
Can I get witcha; visit ya, your place or mine?
Call you on my mobile after seven, use all my free time.
Catch up with the Grapevine
So tell me what's goin' on. . . Let's get it on, hmmm?
Cos you give me that sweetest feeling. When I look at you,
I know what I wanna do. . .

I wanna know you.
I wanna know you. Well?

I wanna know you as good as it gets, like hard knows wet, like I know the alphabet.
A letter at a time, till right on Q, U B mine.
Being frank, giving it to you straight . . .
I wanna do D, F word adjective without statin' the X pletive,
Over and Over. N then. . .
Caress that S timated 36 C chest, with which you have been blessed
Do it from dusk till time T. Have you saying, E Z J, E Z J.
With H and M, phonetically sounding like Hhhh. . .Mmmm
G! One L of a night." Is that OK? Is that alright?
Y? Cos I, wanna make you the VIP,
In my threesome fantasy. Not Tyra, Toni or Naomi.
The threesome will B, W. . . and single me.
U R my desire.

I wanna know you,
I wanna know you well.

I WANNA KNOW YOU

Time

Time the great healer, time the revealer,
Time the constant variable that we each have to consider
The universal denominator, the limiting factor.
That's always moving threatening to catch ya.
Time calibrated in various ways
Centuries, decades, years, months, weeks and days
Hours, minutes, seconds, micro, macro, nano, Chrono, Seiko, Casio
How do measure the length of a moment? On an hour glass with fine sand?
On a wall clock? What is the instant between the tick and the toc?
A sun dial? Define the while it takes to. . .
Relieve writers block.

It's all a matter of time. Once upon a time, just in time, living on borrowed time
World record time, the first time the last time, this time next time one more time
Stand the test of time it gets better with time like a fine wine
Half time, extra time, full time. . . Bedtime? What do you mean time of the month?
You say that every time!

If there were an "Old Father Time" he'd have to be white right?
Cos time is something Black folk can't keep!
It's the gauge of a good nights sleep
The working week, when the next meal is due to eat.
The test of our faith, endurance and perseverance
The parameter of our memory.
Time the deliverer of what is to be, the recorder of history
Her story, my story, our story
Mother Father Sister Brother, what is your plan over time short term or longer.
Do you know what time it is?

Cos time is the constant variable that we each have to consider,
The universal denominator, the limiting factor.
It's always moving, threatening to catch ya
I'm outta time.

Time's up!

TIME

Ignorance Ain't Bliss

When I was a child, I used to think; pretty girls didn't break wind
I thought I was sure to go to Heaven, even though I sinned
Didn't understand why my mom said, "don't talk to strangers, ever!"
Didn't think two men would get married in church. Never!
Now that I'm older, still known as Junior
I know I gotta pray for salvation, to Christ my saviour.
And that such things as hate and real evil exists
That you can't get pregnant from a French kiss.
Otherwise by now the names of my children would make a long list.
Yeah one sure thing I've come to learn is this
Ignorance ain't bliss.

Do you manifest or recognise this trait?
You may feel, I got no material, so I'm just fuelling the debate,
Of another conspiracy theory. Like we are living the movie, "Enemy of the State."
This ain't mild paranoia. To back my reasoning, at this juncture,
I have a few questions for ya.
Do you subscribe to old wives tales?
Did you give up your details to those suppliers of junk e-mails?
Have you got a 25 year mortgage?
Did you know the very word is a euphemism for financial bondage?
Hello! You don't need a third eye to see it.
I hear ya kissing ya teeth, shrugging and saying "cha 'llow it"
Not stopping for a minute to think of how it, could affect you cos now it's
Too controversial, too deep, too sensitive, it could cause a row it's
Your groove, your MO so live and let live? Well that's your choice.
But, I bid you, heed my voice. You can't afford to dismiss my hypothesis.
Ignorance ain't bliss?

Is your comfort zone, bordered by ignorance?
Does it feed your racial intolerance, your own culpable negligence?
Your short sighted lack of appreciation of consequence?
Are you limited with your own lack of experience?
Your readiness to accept things as mere coincidence?
You think it was the really stupid that, created artificial intelligence?
It takes diligence. There is a rewarder of those who diligently seek.
And as I speak I pause for reverence. In reference, to he,
Through whom, you can be delivered from your circumstance.
If I've evoked your spiritual conscience, then that's a bonus to the relevance
The remit, the aim, the mission, the objective, of this piece, which was, which is this
To decree, dispel and state the contrary. Verily, verily, the point you must not miss. .
Ignorance ain't bliss!

You see Ignorance pays no respect to colour, creed or gender
Is found in Mother, Father Sister and Brother
Is the first cousin of complacency,
Illegitimate child of apathy and auntie to indifference,
Raised by Miss Education, a single parent.
Originally from the state of knowledge, Ignorance then went
To rent, a flat in a block called Ivory Towers, in a community known as " Fools Paradise"
Which non-relatively speaking, as neighbourhoods go is quite nice.
And yes true to the proverb, its taken a community to raise this child.
Where Ignorance still resides and has now grown.
Living next-door to Mr Pertunity and now has two seed of its own,
Low-expectation and Laziness. One boy, with an in-bred little sis'.
This is the relative theory of Ignorance. Does it sound like bliss?

Jacqui of all Trades

Jacqui of all trades is a product of the times. Jacqui is fine,
Stands out like Burberry plaid.
She holds her head up like she wears a crown.
Jacqui may have a cream coffee, mahogany, or a nutmeg brown skin tone
A striking mix between a Tyra and a Toni, with a little Naomi, You know.
Jacqui may smoke those low tars and lights maybe a little hash
Hipsters show her figure just right. I seen many a Brotha get whiplash,
Turning their heads, trying to check out Jacqui's stash.
She wears her hair sassy short a weave or micro-braids
Jacqui's looks are doing it for me but I ain't doing it for her. You see though I'm paid
I say what I see, not what she necessarily wants to hear
So she don't appreciate me or keep me near
Through fear that she becomes exposed,
You see I'm different from what she knows
The life she lives and of what she don't know she is afraid
Y'all know Jacqui of all Trades.

Jacqui ain't necessarily your classic gold digger, tart, bimbo, ho... No
She could be academically smart like one woman I know
She could look the part. Work in retail, in the city, be a hustler with a college degree
She could be a mother good or bad, of a child that's treasured
From a marriage that's present, or best not remembered.
To Jacqui it's all just a game she don't feel no shame
But then who's to blame for Jacqui's body trading, morality fadin,
Ain't nothing; but a thing to get laid in her mind
If there's a demand there's a market but guys with no substance spoil it
With their visual displays and slack ways of acquiring and using money
These days forget chivalry times have changed
Jacqui expects, the house your money and the keys to the Lex or the Range
Jacqui wouldn't recognise Goodman if it was her surname
I know your game, Jacqui of all Trades

See I'd like to save Jacqui, me and my rescue complex
Try to show her an alternative flex
From leading suckers on while they run up their credit cards and write big cheques
For the promise, or premise of purchased sex, for a shopping trip or a Rolex
Tell me Jacqui just what is the last Taboo if to you it's all just sex?
Cos it makes me vex, the way you accept those unspoken token
Indecent proposals playing a game with no rules to be broken
Just your fine imprint on an unwritten contract
It ain't just morals but also spirituality that you lack
I say what I mean and I mean what I say when I say
I don't play that's why I wont be played
By you Jacqui of all Trades

But what makes you a Jacqui of all Trades? Beaten by a former lover
That may have been a hopeless brother or father to your child?
Your baby father that don't know how to be a dad?
Or rather maybe you never knew your dad.
Or you did but he treated you so bad?
But is that really legitimate reason
For your legs being open season, to the next payer/player?
Even if you ain't giving it up Jacqui, why do you deliberately use sex as a commodity
To manipulate minds and emotions, cos you choose to, cos you can?
Check yourself Jacqui. If you are truly independent,
Go ahead pay for your own trips to Paris, NY and Milan.
You lie on the bed you make, so don't let me hear you slating the Black man.
These are the observations of the spade who calls a spade
Out to you if you are, or if you know, Jacqui of all Trades.

Hey Ms Dark and Lovely

Hey Ms Dark and Lovely? I've been scoping you for a while
I've been held, captured, by your style, your smile
Your symmetry, your ebony and hmmm, your beautiful Nubian profile.
Yeah I'm sorry, my mother did teach me it's rude to stare but I swear,
You were cast from my rib, so now you definitely ain't spare.
And even if my mother was here today, she would agree
She would praise me in my native tongue
Like, okare omo. Sho mo? Girl you got to be the one.
Cos if I took you to my village, my people would surely kill a cow.
So can we get together sometime, someplace, somehow?

If love is blind, then I best order a white cane and a Labrador
Then I could read you like Braille, easing my fingers so gently over your
Smooth black bumps.
I'll be your number one male fan, sending you fan mail
Telling you exactly how it felt, with nothing mis-spelt
Cos to a word, you are so clearly defined, underlined
Bold capitals in italics, crystal clear and emphatic
But do I read you right? Maybe I'm just dyslexic?

But I get this impression, oh yeah I am impressed
That you are so dark and down and ain't afraid to express
All that culture and identity, well hey baby
That's OK with me but maybe
You like your man, rougher, taller or a lighter shade of brown.
Can I compensate with a date and maybe drive you around this town.
We could work from nought to sixty, cruise on auto drive
And if you wanna know, yeah I got a nine to five.
I could show you my power steering, but I'm also sensitive and caring
And if we move too fast, then I can slow it down with my mellow smooth A.B.S.
Or is that B.A.S.S.?
Maybe I am dyslexic.
But I'll ask again Miss Dark and Lovely just to make it stick.
Can we get together sometime, someplace, somehow?

HEY MS DARK & LOVELY

Smoove Like What?

Smoove like a horn note from Satchimo?
Smoove like Baileys chilled and thick, you know.
Smoove like Jill Scott got flow. Like how Me'shell Ndegeocello, blows alto.
Smooth like a Joe, Chico or D'Angelo mid tempo?
Smoove like a gear change on a Volvo?
Smoove like a Lynden or Maxwell jam?
Smoove like pounded yam, made in the village. . ?
Is it just my words, or you referring to the whole package?
Don't you realise that Junior is Da Imej, on stage or not?
You say my words are "smoove". . . I wanna know, smoove like what?

Smoove huh?
After Livin' in Stonebridge and then Nigeria,
I could get down like a regular street nigga.
But I got nuthin to prove, I've taken the rough with the smoove.
You know what I've been through to wear a white collar?
If I spent more time witcha,
You'd see what you call smoove, is just my nature.
It ain't a front, it's just my MO
But I don't understand, I don't know.
How ya mean smoove? Is it like Luther, or an Eighties rare groove?
Well you check yourself, you know what you got.
A saying springs to mind, 'bout a kettle and a pot.
So tell me, smoove like what?

Smoove like the way your cheekbones accentuate your eyes
Smoove like the hairless skin on your thighs, hmmm?
Go ahead; take a moment to verify.
....
Have you taken a while? You bustin' loose that smoove smile?
Are my words that smoove? OK maybe not.
Can you fill me in, smoove like what?
Smoove like the way your rich black hair lays on your head
Smoove like melted butter on bread?
Smoove like Carte Dor? A'ight how 'bout Hagen Dazs instead,
Melting on your tongue?
Smoove like Brian McKnight croons, "You could be the one."
My words are nothing if they ain't real.
My words are an extension of the way that I feel.
The way that I feel, three words?
Nah, I'll prevaricate and use dots.
. . . Smoove like what?

SMOOTH LIKE WHAT?

If I Could

If I could, I'da caught the bullets that killed Malcolm and Martin,
Then traced them back to the individuals that pulled the strings of the puppets
That owned the fingers that pulled the triggers.
If I could, I'd like to meet the first person to call us niggers.
If I could, I'd give Nelson back his twenty seven years.
And for the families of Stephen Lawrence and Michael Menson, I'd ease their tears.
Cos they're just two of the daily victims of racial attacks
And I'm supposed to think the police commissioner and the system got my back?
I don't see it like that.
Just cos some faceless Mr McPherson says so, oh, now it's official,
Yeah there is institutionalised racism but hello, it ain't new to me at all
If I could, I'd make the Queen pay taxes,
I'd take that big ass purple stone in her crown, you know the amethyst,
I'd sell it and settle the third world debt crisis. . .If I could.

If I could, I'da seen Earth Wind and Fire live.
I'd wear an Afro like the Jackson Five
I'da recorded an album with Stevie and I'da given TLC a Grammy for Unpretty.
If I could I'da watched Ali had a ringside seat to the Thriller in Manila.
If I could I'da been Marciano's forty eighth opponent
And given him a forty seven and one record.
If I could, I'da flown like Jordan with the Bulls,
Won the "3peat", in fact scored the winning basket in 97, with a crossover and a Jam
If I could I'd play mixed doubles with Venus, clean sweep the Grand Slam, then celebrate like damn!
If I could I'd make Tiger Woods stand in front of the Ku Klux Klan
And have him explain to them just how he ain't a Black Man. . .If I could.

If I could I would name and shame the sell-outs today
I have a list so I'ma do that anyway.
Ease their amnesia one generation after getting here
Forgetting where they are from. lost in suits, brogues, and a tie.
All those who psychologically masturbate, selling their conscience for an hourly rate
Living the ultimate lie.
I don't care who you are or how much you earn.
The average wage and awareness of the Black Man is still near nil.
If I could do something about that. . . .I can, so I will.
If I could I'd send some Sistas home for recognition of cultural values
I'd send some Brothas back home to acquire some drive to be whatever they choose
I'd send the coconuts home never to return again
And I'd send some white folk home to get a picture of my pain
And Walk in My Black Shoes.

If I could change my life, tonight I'd be going home to a beautiful Black Wife
Then we'd get up to the mischief that might just make my first son
And she'd say "Junior baby beau. . . You da man Hon"
This after improvising on the love makin'
Being careful not to wake my Louise and Jasmine,
Then getting' up in the mornin' crusty eyed and yawnin'
Looking forward to a better day for Brothas and Sistas,
Black people plural not just the individual but the collective
And I wouldn't need to worry about the future, nor rue the retrospective
If I could. . . But then maybe I would
Not have precipitated all the character and passion to express myself in this fashion
So if that's the case and I changed things, would it be for the good?
Even if I could.

IF I COULD

How's the family?

**My Little Brother. . . Damilola, stabbed and killed. For me, what compounded the tragedy?
Was the fear that the culprits were possibly my other little Brothers.
Some say the Black kids like that need education and counselling, true.
I say give it to their fathers and mothers
Cos it's been taught, self hate ingrained especially if you have a funky African name
I know that cos in the playground I suffered the same,
Animosity towards my identity. And even then, it was my brothers who were dogging me.
Why? Cos of a lack of cohesive identity, cos of what history has imposed on we
Here we are 21st Century. White folks, got theirs, Asians made theirs
And Black folk still think it's cool to be late.
Well it ain't my destiny, it ain't my fate.
My little Sisters . . . The illegitimate children of destiny
Now have misguided misplaced icons in their face, of what a woman should be
Even Lauren admits her mis-education. So the role models have to be, today's parents you and me.
Cos we hold the answer to the question
How's the family.**

**My Parents. . . They warned me years ago. Said I should watch my back
But I was young. . .Though gifted and Black. Thought I was cool, excelling in school,
Academics sports and athletics, too young to understand, too young to know.
See they arrived here by invitation, encountered a less subtle mode of racism
In the land of the colonial master.
Had their minds messed with, so they went back about 20 years after
By then, the Empire had labelled the colonies the Common wealth . . . commonly broke
On the brink of civil wars famine and disaster
But we don't do any better when we're given our own countries to look after.
Why? Greed! Black mans inability to distinguish desire from need
That's our problem. And those who run the system what about them?
Well now cos I ain't doin'10 second 100 metres or faster, or an entertainer with a white partner
I'm experiencing the same things my parents went through, yeah experience is a good teacher
In some ways I'm a chip of the old block. But the chip is seen as on my shoulder
By the authorities that run the system that limits me, well what do you see?
How is the family?**

**My Sisters . . . Now first and second generation graduates.
Some recognise the glass ceilings, but there are others that fuel the debate.
Losing touch with the X and Y axis of their success.
Seduced by this Eurocentric tribal mess that demands that you remember to forget
Who you are and take up Black man berating.
Eliminating, cultural values, and customs like self respect
It's become a lifestyle thing. I think my sisters shed too much just to fit in.
Abandoning natural looks to get the weave in. Forgetting their heritage and origins.
No disrespect to your achievements but it's been done before and it's happening again
Deflate and suppress the credibility of the Black man your natural husband and partner
What's a family without its natural leader? Sisters we need a little more love from ya
A little investing in our call to be the best that we can be.
Otherwise you have no right to ask how is the family?**

My Brothers. . . Are you younger versions of older me?
Do you look to the future and wonder how it will be
If all the hopefully Mr Rights keep doing wrong.
Mis- Representing and turning out to be uncle Toms
Will our children yours and mine have watered down cultures and diluted minds?
Cos the imminent European education curriculum
Would rather teach how homosexuality is cool, than educate how my ancestry is African.
We have a collective responsibility for self education, historical motivation, collective elevation
So Bro please start educating and being there for your seed if you ain't
Teach them that Black skin is not just an exotic lick of paint
I don't accept an incapacity for recollection, I seek acceptance not assimilation
Our heritage some wanna trivialise it, our look, the same people wanna acquire it.
Our culture don't put a price on it and let them hire it!
In my day and time, in your day and time, in this day and time
The true answer should be just fine, when I'm asked
How's the family?

But it ain't. When will it be?

Sorry, I make no Apologies

I make no apologies, for being brown skinned and dark as I am,
For taking a shine, to fine Black Women,
Especially those with a darker shade of tan.
I make no excuses for my own choices;
I accept them, as every adult should and can.
Cos my experiences and their consequences make me the man that I am . . .
Second born son of Ola Dimeji
The Video Guy, I may not be, yeah I feel ya India Irie!

I make no apologies that when it comes to Garage music. . .
I'd never ask for more! Cos I can't stand it!
Do I look like Oliver? But the Artful Dodger?. .A'ight, I can 'llow it.
I make no apologies for my shaving bumps,
My subtle funk, being 5'10", so I can barely dunk
For being verbally aggressive, yet sensitive,
Hating smoking, whether low tar, cigar or spliff.

No apologies for speaking my mind, sometimes loving blind.
Though noticing when I'm being taken for a ride, just cos I'm being kind
For never voting, my style of joking,
I got love for Will Smith cos he's cool and don't swear, are you miffed?
I ain't into DMX, are you vexed? Whatever!
For my love of R'n'B, Soul, Jazz, and a little Hip-Hop in no particular order
And so what if I ain't much of a dancer?
I'm sorry, I make no apologies.

I make no apologies for being the father of two beautiful girls
I ain't just a baby father a mere biological vector.
I'm a dad/provider and they're a. . . . Major part of my world.
Now to my legibility, whether you consider that, a pro-viso, but or a plus.
It's reality baby! Ain't just about you and me, it's about family. It's about we, it's about us.
I make no apologies for imparting cultural discipline
From my heritage, cos it's instilled deep within.
No apologies for the need to impress this, to my princesses,
The importance of respect, education, behaving right and correct.
And if they didn't, it's still my right, despite not being PC and the law,
To tell them what for, then give them a good beating.
I ain't ever had to yet! See my girls are good. So something's right in my teaching.

No apologies for being particular about domestic hygiene.
Teaching them to live clean, plaiting hair and greasing knees.
Talking with my daughters about virtues, values and priorities
I accept my responsibilities, giving hugs and squeezes, kisses in public
Being an exception to the negative statistics.
So that they can have things that I never had.
You think I'm strict? You shoulda seen my dad,
Sorry, I make no apologies

I make no apologies for declaring Jesus as Lord and saviour,
The only redeemer for my bad behaviour,
Cos God made Da imej in his image
And any good work he started, he will be faithful and will complete it.
Too bad if this proclamation of my faith offends you, I won't delete it.
I'm sorry. . . I make no apologies.

The Essence of Life

I showed up at the hospital for a routine ultra –sound.
The pathologist took me aside cos something irregular was found
"It appears that there's a serious blood disorder
That could be life threatening to your unborn daughter"
I'm thinking Jasmine my baby, not even a flower just a bud
An innocent party, sweet thing my flesh my blood.

Doc tells me 'bout counselling and termination
I said," No way I've been looking forward to a celebration
Of the gift of life and that's what my girl will live
I don't know much about blood but my group is B positive
So positive is what I will be". I shut out the thoughts of negativity
But at the door of my mind knocked reality.

My fly friend Adele has suffered from birth. I asked her "How do you cope with this"?
She said Junior it ain't easy , one day I'm fine, the another a bad crisis. . .
I've got a disability that ain't obvious to see. . . I'm always fatigued
It's so hard to be understood or even believed.

I'm deformed not the norm. 'Look nice on the outside, when my hair's done you seen me
Yet inside I feel I let people down and I'm so unpretty
Blighted by something to which no cure has been found.
With my internal organs, my life, threatened by deficient blood flowing 'round.

And in my silent screams, condense pain streams. I'm afraid one day one day I'll drown in the flood
I begin to get the picture and think to myself," is this the legacy I've given my little girl
My flesh my blood"?
But through my fly friend Adele though all is not well, I sense her positive spirit despite her strife
I focus on that and realise the human spirit is the essential essence of life.

It turned out that the diagnosis was a wrong call
And my baby was fine after all
Now Jasmine's well, despite the odd graze after a fall, though still nothing more that a bud
I truly appreciate her health, the essence of life. My daughters, my flesh my blood.

THE ESSENCE OF LIFE

Northern Line Exposure

Recently changed my route to the 9 to 5.
The Jubilee line had extensive works on the southbound trek.
So I switched to the Northern line through Colindale.
Had some personal reservations, based on my recent past but
. . . what the heck.
It's Wednesday. I Cased the regulars for that 8.10 Bank train.
Like clock-work, there's that fine, braided sister again.
Three days runnin', gotta be routine for her! Reason enough
To make it routine for me. . .

Can't even begin to imagine it going down like Craig David's "Seven Days."
No discredit to the boys prowess of persuasion but she had to be a slapper anyway.
Could you put that scenario down to teenage hormones on a rage?
Well I was never that way inclined, at any age.
Ain't a phase I was once in and out of which I've now grown.
Nah always had an M.O. of my own. . .
Just get my nought to sixty on, nuthin' too strong, who knows, she could be the one too..

She paced along the platform from my left.
Her aura hit me 'bout 10 paces before her scent, spicy and light,
I recognised it. . . 212 for men?
My head rotated slowly though 180 degrees till she stopped on my right.
Hunt up wind, Rule number one in the game. Damn! Now she must be clocking my cologne.
While I'm thinkin', what I'd like to do, what I might do, do right, so right.

Then maybe we could jam, like that old school Isley Brothers record that Pops used to loop on a Sunday morn, or "Papa Was a Rolling Stone."
Ah yeah the Temptations, the temptation, the temptation. . . .

She clocked me on her left as she flipped a page in her Essence magazine.
Held up the front cover, as I blew mine. The Bank train pulled into the station.
The cover caption for the feature read "How to Love a Black Man."
Lady, could I be your teacher?

Oh Yeah, that was my train but curiosity,
That thing that got the cat, might just work for me.
What insight was she
Gettin' from the editorial. Was it enhancing at all,
What she already knew. How wide was her research?
Were there many or few, was there a queue?
Maybe she was learning what she didn't previously understand
And maybe. . . I could offer a tutorial or a hand.

As I stepped closer she purred at a picture of Morris what's-his-name.
I wasn't fazed, see I got a tight talk game.

"Couldn't help noticing the cover. How to love a Black Man."
"Sorry", she replied with her best effort to feign any awareness of my attention.
"Oh, oh yeah. Is there a Black Man that you want to love?" I didn't flinch.
"Er no, no. I'm straight. And judging by the way you're ogling that picture you're straight too. Or at least swing both ways." She laughed, we laughed, ice broken.

"Hmmmph." Her mischievous acknowledgement served as encouragement.
"Hmmmph what, the latter or the former?" She looked directly at me for the first time in our encounter.
"What do you think?"
"I know what I'd like to think. Damn I certainly know! But mamma used to say never judge a book by the cover. I'd like to think that you're straight. Having said that, as a straight guy, talking to a woman he finds attractive, I would say that wouldn't I?
On the flip side your scent, 212 for men? Could that be throwing me off scent?
What I think and what is, may well differ."

A pause, to gather her things or maybe her thoughts as her Charing Cross train eased into the station.

"You know what I think?" She replied
"What do you think?"
"I think you missed your Bank train"

The question unanswered my curiosity still aroused.
Tried to play it off and checked how many minutes to the next Bank Train...
3. ..2...1...2 for men, hmmm.

Thursday, pulled a sickie. You know how we do. Damn I'm due for a break and a rise.
Had a lay in with Wednesday mornings encounter on my mind.

Friday; arrived extra early for that Bank train, picked up the Metro
Browsed on yesterday's news and the horoscopes. Didn't tell me anything I didn't know.
But I noticed that Sis again. Same braids, no pumps but a pair of low black mules.
Still looking fly, in her dress down Friday mode.
Where previously there was Essence, there was Fridays Metro... Same aura though.
Waited 10 paces, inhaled... different scent. Still light, this time the fresh side of spicy, The feminine side of the swing. My head did the 180 degree thing.
And I proceeded to pour gently, cos broken ice can sometimes make an awkward splash.

"How's it goin'?"
"Southbound via Charing Cross as usual? And yours is the Bank train right?"
Splash! Ice water everywhere. Chilled, I began to mop up the mess.

"So you've been watching me huh?"
"There's a difference between noticing and watching."
"Like tasting and eating perhaps?"
"Perhaps." She looked at me again, seemingly seeking verification that our wavelengths were the same. Nought to sixty was in effect mode. I stepped up my talk game.

"Yeah there's options as to how I get to work, different moods different ways.
I just have to go South to get there. Yeah it's all about going South, right?
Change the route like you may change your scents, to suit those different moods perhaps?
On that note Allure becomes you..."

She smiled humoured; I sense more by my knowledge of scents, than my subtle innuendo.

"So what makes a woman wear a mans cologne?"
"Well. Ambience, the smell and yeah, the different moods, like you said."

"So you bought it for yourself, or is it residual from your man's collection?"
"I don't have a man, don't want a man, don't need a man!"

Ice water from a cannon! The plot thickened, now the swing definitely had a slant.
My mind begins to imagine her going south... Nah surely she can't.

"That's a strong blanket statement to make. If you don't mind me saying.
I've been hurt before but tshhh, still need a woman. Didn't that Essence you had on Wednesday give you a new angle on how to?"
She gave me a look that would have reduced any cats' lives considerably.
...If looks could kill. I decided to let curiosity lie.

But another of Pops old jams, Marvin's "What's Going On" was on cue.
My mind begged the question.
Was she lesbian, Bi or fresh out of a bad relationship with a guy?
I switched the flow as her Charing Cross train came in.

"So er, what do you do anyway?"
"I'm a corporate lawyer in the City" She strut her stuff, recomposed.
"No shit?"
"No shit, what about you?"
I replied just before the train doors closed
"I work on a cologne concession at Boots."

Walk in My Black Shoes

da imej

Walk in My Black Shoes

The complexities of possessing dual cultures can be frustrating. Living in an environment that subtly demands that the predominant part of those dual cultures is denounced, remains a constant issue amongst the diverse spectrum of young culturally embracing, aspiring professionals in London.

"Walk in My Black Shoes" breaks it down. The influences of racism, history, politics, sexism and oppression, are reflected in this first novel. Illustrating how a web of friends and associates in their early 20's express, suppress, compromise and slander their respective cultural influences. In the conscious decisions they make and those that are imposed upon them by the system.

Deoye Olaiya is the central character around whom the web is spun. Having been born in England before moving back to Nigeria with his family for over a decade, he returns to London independently as a young Black man. Clear on his identity as a Nigerian but equally ready to claim his rights as a British Citizen. Deoye is tormented by the success of his professional footballer best friend and the hardships he suffered in Nigeria but appreciates that they have defined his character and his ambition to succeed. Around him influences from other friends/associates of West Indian, Middle Eastern, Indian, English and Nigerian descent, have sway on his relationships, motivation and frustrations. Deoye walks in his father's black shoes experiencing new things and parallels that his father had endured when he came to London some thirty years before. He contends with his perceptions and the chip that resides on his shoulder, as he tries to walk a different route.

Amane Al-Shifa is rich. In compassion, culture and wealth. The only daughter of a Kuwaiti oil player, Amane fights to forge her own identity. Breaking out of the stereotypes and cultural restrictions, that may come with being from a fundamentally Islamic background. With her proud father, overbearing sexist brother and an insecure boyfriend Amane seeks support and understanding from society and her flat mates who each have their own cultural wranglings; these spill over into their relationship as Amane tries to retain her independence and her friendships. Her elegant black shoes are no easier to walk in.

Afolabi Shokoya is the negative stereotype of a Nigerian fraudster living in London. His justification; payback for colonial exploitation. Shokoya worked his legal stay with an arranged marriage. He dabbles in hoax benefit claims, credit card fraud, drugs and 419 (Nigerians own-patented brand of rip off), to finance his expensive taste, with St. John's Wood flat, designer labels and no remorse. Now the hustler turned player, is being played by his ex-wife, Sheresse, who in turn is being extorted, by her wannabe Yardie Baby Father. Sheresse struggles to lay a clearer path for her daughter to follow as a single parent. Shokoya contrives to stay one step ahead of the system, wearing out much leather on his designer shoes as he does so.

It takes time to adjust to someone else's shoes. You need to break them in, to stretch them out and to adapt... Some people may find them too uncomfortable and give up. Some of us will persevere, empathize and gain inspiration or warning as we step with the characters in their Black Shoes.

Walk in My Black Shoes

Junior Ola Dimeji

Prologue

"C'mon! I must have more change somewhere." Deoye stressed out loud as he threw another pair of fruitless jeans on his bed. He was broke to his last bronzes and had only managed to gather forty nine pence from the clothes that he had shaken down. Made up of copper two pence pieces and a few silver five pence coins. He left the heaps of one pence pieces in his coin jar alone. These were reserved for the extreme cases and having been in this position before, he didn't consider this to be extreme. Difficult yes, but not extreme.

Deoye dug his long fingers into the front pocket of his last pair of jeans, no joy. He kissed his teeth and deepened his seemingly ever present grimace, glanced at his Casio wrist watch and threw the trousers onto the bed.

"2.45p.m. I' got fifteen minutes to sign on, he continued his thoughts. I could do without this. I ain't a bum. I've got a lot to offer but here I am, broke like a joke! Struggling to make up train fare from Colindale to Hendon Central, one stop, eighty pence, so sad." Again, Deoye kissed his teeth and shook his head as he drew out the disapproving gesture. He begun folding the mass of clothes on the bed and putting them back into the wardrobe, meticulously taking his time to fold each garment and hang or shelve them individually. As he pivoted to his right each time to put his garm's away, he faced the full length mirror fixed inside his wardrobe door he paused momentarily to critically survey his reflection.

At just short of six foot, Deoye was big boned and muscular. A lean twelve stone but deceptively bigger than he appeared when fully clothed. Naturally athletic, he took much pride in his physical presentation and worked hard to stay in shape. He was lean and subtly cut from a moderate but consistent work out regime. He looked down at his hands and smirked as he turned them over, registering the ever present blisters where palm meets finger, brought about by almost religious daily curl reps. He took a moment to put in his black onyx spade earring. "Gotta keep it real and represent" He murmured rubbing his jaw. He felt two days bristle and stepped closer to the mirror. Checking out the inward growing hairs he sighed again.

Deoye was real enough to concede that he never considered himself as being, handsome. Dark, with very pronounced features a constantly furrowed brow and thick lips. He thought his profile was his best feature and accepted that some people may find his physical appearance intimidating, black or white. "Damn I need a fade." He observed, commenting on the overgrowth of his short cut hair while stepping back from the mirror. He reached for a blue Nike cap and pulled it down low on his head and once more looked in the mirror. The most obvious flaw on his body, just a below his left clavicle a two inch diagonal scar. Deoye focused on the blemish while subconsciously running his left thumb along the wound.

Trying to shut out the memory of how the wound came about long ago, but remembered like yesterday, the result of the beating of his life from his dad. Attempting to focus on the physical reflections the mirror presented behind him of his influences, role models and five of his favourite women photographs and posters, from magazines, stuck to the inside of the opposite wardrobe door. Will Smith, Mohammed Ali, Michael Jordan, Denzel Washington the guys and Tyra Banks, Venus Williams, Nia Long, Lauren Hill and Denise Lewis, the babes. All chosen for different reasons some shallow and superficial some deeper.

He saw the guys as icons of sports and entertainment, keeping it real. Black and down yet still successful. While the women, his favourite five, Black strong and beautiful. What he lacked was a mentor come role model as a young black man in England in the professional realms outside of sports and entertainment with the same credibility.

He reached inside the wardrobe to grab a denim shirt and glanced in the mirror again. Whilst slipping the shirt over his torso he caught yet another glimpse of the wound, inducing another long sigh. Another time check 2.47pm. " Let's go Black man, gotta catch this signing on gig" he thought. As memories of growing up came back to play again, he completed putting the last of his clothes away.

****

Tidiness was an attribute that, along with general domestic awareness, Deoye had been taught by his late mother who died when he was just sixteen. She raised her two children well, while making a positive financial contribution to the household budget by succeeding professionally, being a loving parent who gave all to make sure her children's priorities were right . . . God first, then education and all the rest to follow. Often, as Deoye was going through his early teens he would have a moral abberation. He'd first encounter his mom's wrath when news of his misdeeds reached home.

A fair disciplinarian, Abeke Olaiya was a Yoruba woman from the old school mold. She knew all the traditional fables and idioms to use when appropriating punishment to her stubborn son. The reciting of which prolonged the anticipation of the imminent beating or sanction and could have you in tears long before she had actually appropriated the punishment .The biggest torment was when she would begin reciting one of those old proverbs up to the last line, then ask Deoye to complete it and deliver the punchline, thus giving him a moments insight to what the nature of his punishment would be. Deoye learnt duly that pretending not to know what the end of such proverbs were, as that would warrant an extra beating for not listening . . . twice.

Respect is a great cornerstone of Nigerian culture. In Yoruba traditions it is more elaborate. Deoye and his elder sister Bolanle, four years his senior, learnt the fundamentals of their culture long before they left England with their parents back to Nigeria. Both parents made points of speaking the mother tongue to their children as they raised them in England in the mid to late seventies before the family returned to Nigeria in 1984. While they were taught the intricacies of greetings, for all times of the day, special regards for their elders, asking directions and yes all of those proverbs by Mum, they picked up much of how to hold their own in abuse and insults from their father Bolaji Olaiya.

Abeke was also heralded in the community for her culinary skills. There wasn't a Yoruba dish that she didn't cook exceptionally well with her own personal accent on it. Various rices, stews meat preparations, vegetable dishes . . .Whatever "Iya Bolanle" (Bolanle,s mother, parents are referred to as the parent of their first born) knew it well.

General consensus amongst family and in the community, was that she took her cooking to another level and she passed on her skills to her two children. Bolanle learnt well before her twelfth birthday to prepare food for her father up to the standard he had been now spoilt by. Deoye on the other hand, had to be dragged to the kitchen by his ear from the age of eight and learnt the basics of cooking at the kitchen sink . . . Washing plates and pots. His mother would say; "Adeoye if you like to eat the food, you'd better learn to cook the food and that starts with washing up!"

Deoye was a quick learner though. Constantly encouraged by the free sample morsels to be gained by being near the pots and pans in the kitchen, he was able to cook most intricate dishes by the time he was fifteen. Though he didn't quite get to spend enough time with his mother to learn how to cook his favourite crab and vegetable stew, Deoye loved his food and always use to joke with his mom that in the future his prospective wife would have to attend courses and training on how Mamma use to make it. In response she'd encourage him, "You're getting good enough to teach anyone yourself, its just patience timing and doing things in the right proportions and knowing what goes with what."

Many a time Deoye would creep to the kitchen at night having witnessed the preparation of regular beef stew, that everyday concoction in Nigerian households that Mom masterly prepared, consisting of ground tomatoes, pepper, onions with meat, stock, groundnut oil and various herbs, spices and seasonings and help himself to a chunk of boneless meat, fistsize. The size that is reserved for his father, with a little stew and a wedge of bread for a midnight snack and so aid restful sleep. He was rarely caught in the act but was convinced his mother had a sixth sense of knowing exactly how many pieces of meat were actually in each pot without physically counting them. Abeke Olaiya knew and on the occasion she caught her son with saucepan lid in one hand and dripping beef chunk in the other it wasn't easy for him. Rather than shouting at 2.30 a.m., she calmly looked at him told him to put the meat on a saucer, closed the pot and go to bed.

Stealing meat from your moms pot of stew is low. Getting caught at it sets you up for ridicule for the rest of your life. Relatives you have never met would refer to you as the one who stole the meat from the pot. The fear of the punishment kept Deoye awake the rest of that night. When the fateful moment came for him to learn what his punishment was, sure enough the prelude was a short sermon about wrongs and rights featuring one or two Yoruba proverbs with the basic moral of each, along the lines of "thou shall not steal."From his mother, Deoye received a relatively light beating and was banished to his room . . . till his father arrived home. That's when Deoye wished he could turn back time.

He was beaten so thoroughly with koboko (dried goat skin leather with eight strands each a metre long) all over his body head and all. When he finally went to bed that night he began to seriously doubt if he was the true son of his father. It was late on a Saturday after noon when his dad had returned home that day and as usual he had been drinking socially but did that justify calling his son "Omoale, Omoale!" (bastard, bastard) repeatedly, while he was administering the beating of his sons life?

Deoyes mother returned with his sister Bolanle from a visit to family friends in the evening to check on him. No doubt the gist of his meat thieving had been spread. He considered how he was ever going to live it down with Tayo and Funmi. They were his closest friends and because of their closeness were referred to as cousins. No doubt his mother, if not his sister had spread the gist.

On her way up the stairs, his mother noticed specks of blood. Trying to dismiss it for a nose bleed which her son was prone to having, she knew the husband she had and feared worse. As she opened her sons bedroom door she called his name.

"Adeoye"

"Ma!"he answered hoarsely and got up off the bed to prostrate and apologise to his mother. Wearing just jeans, his body was latticed in whelts and deep bloody cuts from the whipping he had received.

"I am sorry mummy for stealing meat from the pot."

The apology hadn't registered, his Mother looked down at him sorrowfully, shaking.

Deoye looked up at his mum having noticed she had not acknowledged the apology and repeated it. "I'm sorry Mummy."

"Ssshh, Ma se be mo omo mi, pele pele." (don't do it again my child, sorry, sorry) she whispered with a lump in her throat. She called to her daughter to bring her medical bag. Bolanle arrived in the room to see her brothers head bowed in shame unconcerned with his wounds. As she came closer Bolanle winced at the ugly blisters all over her little brothers body. Abeke and her daughter treated all Deoyes wounds with tears in their eyes. Ninety-two separate scars they dressed. Occasionally sighing at the ferocity that must have been rendered to leave such scars, while Deoye was more embarrassed by the fact that he had done what he had done, been punished for it, now his mom and his sister were weeping while they dressed his wounds with detol solution and vaseline. He felt their genuine anguish and this multiplied his guilt.

Deoye tossed and turned for two hours after his mother and sister left his room. His bed sheet stained in blood as he tried in vain, to minimise the surface area which he lied on. His whole body ached and throbbed. The whelts stung like 92 stubbed toes at the same time. Deoye had just resolved he'd sit up through the night when he heard his sister at the door.

"Deoye." She softly called so as not to alert any attention from her parents room.

"Come in Bola." Deoye had always been a brat of a junior brother to his sister. Often embarrassing her and putting his sizable frame about as he had always been quite big and well built for his age. He was just beginning to respect his sister and appreciate at the age of thirteen, his sisters maturity and the qualities that she had obviously inherited from their mother. Now seeing his sister coming through the door with a plate of food for him and tears in her eyes for him. He knew it was time to grow up and do all possible to put all the sibling rivalry, which he always initiated, well behind him.

"Ah Popsie really showed you Deoye, are you O.K?"

"I can't lie Bola, it hurts bad all over." Bolanle put the pyrex dish containing Jolloff rice down and brought out a packet of paracetamol from her robe pocket

"Here take these." She placed two tablets in her brothers hand and clasped it as he motioned to take them.

"Thanks egbon. (big sister or brother) Thanks for being there for me and I'm sorry for disrespecting you for so long." Bolanle embraced her brother hard and kissed his forehead.

"Aargh Bola!"

"And I thought you were big and mature enough to appreciate a little overt sisterly love hmm?"

"It's not like that big sis, you just squeezed the big one on my chest."

They looked at each other then simultaneously began a little bout of laughter that ended with them both in tears.

"Come on, you'd better eat something." Bolanle admonished. She handed him the pyrex with the rice and the very piece of meat that he wanted to take from the pot night before.

"Eh heh Man and beast meet again, this time you shall not escape my grasp" Deoye joked in a sinister Hammer House of Horror imitation, then proceeded to plunge his teeth, like a starved carnivore into the meat. As he came up for air his sister chuckled.

"Deoye! Who send you steal meat from pot self?" she said in pigeon English as once more she surveyed the damage to her brothers body"

"But the meat sweet oh!" Deoye confessed saluting their mothers cooking prowess yet again. Bolanle didn't retort she just continued looking at her brother lashed body and wondered where her dads sense of proportion was in giving such a beating to her little brother. But their father had never been one for compassion or dialogue.

To the outsider Bolaji Olaiya's positive traits couldn't be seen they were all latent. While he was openly proud of his wifes domestic awareness to outsiders, at home he rarely showed affection or appreciation to anyone. In fact the marks now on Deoye's body gave a greater insight to how Mr Olaiya expressed his emotions. Bolanle shuddered at the thought of what her mother had endured for years as she lightly wrapped a blanket round her brothers beaten body.

Unlike his wife whose objective thinking and reasoning helped her modulate in society and adapt accordingly. Mr Olaiya was a die hard traditionalist. Deoye inherited his persistence from his father who was a very uncompromising man and very proud. The first in his family to complete secondary education, Bolaji was academically brilliant and stayed committed to his professional ambition to become a chartered accountant. Which he finally achieved while in England in ninety seventy eight. He achieved his Institute of Chartered Accountancy certificate at the third time of trying, it took three efforts because he was also juggling marketing and finance certificates while attempting the first two efforts. His wife acknowledged his studying capacity though suggested him to pursue his aspirations over a longer period of time.

Being the traditionalist he was, Bolaji Olaiya thought his wife had over stepped her bounds and should focus her attention on bringing up their two children and concentrate on the archetypal feminine occupation at the time, of Midwifery.

After his first failure, Abeke made her suggestion. Bolaji's pride, already wounded by his first ever academic failure (going back as far as primary school he was always in the top three pupils in whatever subject). Now his wife, the traditionally subservient partner in the marriage, dared to impose her suggestions on him. "A whole first born Olaiya." He would not allow his wife, could not let her overstep her traditional boundaries. It couldn't happen he had to up hold his male pride and make his point . The point was made physically. Thus in the summer of 1976 a history of beatings for Abeke Olaiya begun.

At first an occasional open handed slap was delivered just to mark his territory. Abeke was shocked and hurt more mentally than physically. As an obedient child, one of two brothers and a sister. She wasn't hit at all after the age of seven now twenty five years later, her husband had begun this medieval act.

Shocked and humiliated Abeke didn't reveal her husbands violent conduct to anyone. She hoped that it would turn out to be just a one off loss of control. But control was what her husband sought. Over his family and his social environment. His wifes popularity and social tact he found threatening and undermined his importance as head of the Olaiyas household. Rather than redefining his own self assessment and trying to add attributes which he certainly needed in abundance, he stubbornly stagnated and wanted the world around him to stop developing too.

It offended him that he had left his beloved home land behind. Where just by virtue of being a man he was higher in society than any woman. To come to cold, colonial master England where the only employment he could find eroded his pride. Morale destroying jobs as a hospital porter, road sweeping, cleaning offices and yet encounter racism all in for the cause of a professional education. His whole cultural existance was challenged every day and his traditional world was now limited to the four walls of the rented room that the Olaiya's called home in North West London.

Abeke used to be part of his world, but now "she had grown wings" in the Oyingbos land. She had been listening too much to the liberated women's movements of the sixties and seventies. Wings he would forever be trying to clip. Bolaji begun working on killing his wifes spirit and soon the physical assault was as damaging as the mental torment.

As so many mothers are often torn between staying in an abusive marriage 'for the children's sake' and leaving, the situation is further compounded in Nigerian culture. Women of that era just couldn't up and go. By tradition, the woman truly leaves the parents house . . . And stayed, in sickness or health . . . Or better or for worse . . .

Having returned to Nigeria in nineteen eighty four, Bolaji was on home ground. Customs and traditional ethics generally supported his ideology on marriage and West Africa wasn't quite familiar with the do it all mother, feminism and all of the female awareness movements that had liberated women in the West. Bolaji did not advocate his wife being a pioneer of any such ideals back in Lagos.

The beatings became more frequent as Bolaji visited his home town from Lagos to Ondo, where he was the local champion. The one who travelled to the land of the Oyingbo and read books. He was heralded in his town he could escape the realities of cosmopolitan Lagos, fast pace, hustle bustle, congested streets slow moving traffic and all. Where he felt , pressured, threatened and out of control.

His wife thrived and continued to advance, socially and professionally. Leaving mainstream nursing to become an industrial nurse in aprogressive kitchen ware manufacturers. The company was now exporting all over West Africa. Abeke expanded into selling some of the merchandise herself.

She made considerable profits as a reward for her enterprise. Bolaji saw this as a further slight to his male ego and compounded the beatings on his wife. He claimed she insulted him by implying he did not provide enough for his family. By this time Deoye was twelve and in secondary school, while his sister was away in boarding school.

With the physical abuse of his mother taking place in front of him, Deoye regularly endured and often would get a good thrashing for trying to restrain his fathers rage. His mother asked him to forgive his father and not to judge him on what he saw, which he saw too often. Abeke also asked her son not to let his sister know what she was enduring. In an effort to keep her from poisoning her mind against her father. Deoye pledged to his mother that she could confide in him but asked in return that she seriously consider leaving his father.

He couldn't understand his mothers almost suicidal devotion. Abeke held her son close and cried regretting that at such a young age he had stated what she had been contemplating in her mind for a long time. Abeke had told her husband by that time repeatedly,

"Beat me again and I will leave you Bolaji."

That was so long ago and numerous bruises and slaps since. Bolaji, inspired by his native family in Ondo received much back patting for putting Iya Bolanle in her place.

Abekes female inlaws were numerous and obviously jealous of her education but not knowing anything else, too readily accepted the role of domestic wife that is seen not heard. Being that she was from Ibadan a very academically inclined city, she had a exceptionally strong educational influence from her parents and all her siblings had further education. Which was a contrast to her husbands family where he alone amongst his fathers twelve children from three wives, managed to break the mode of farming, taxi driving or manual labour. They wished their champion had married a local girl and set about setting up a second wife that they could manipulate and monitor. Bolaji was all for the idea of having a hometown girl who would worship him without challenging his mind. The way it was for his brothers and his fore fathers. The man assumed the role as leader by virtue of having a penis.

After screening a number of impressionable girls from the local vicinity, aided by his brothers connections. Bolaji managed to snare a local girl, Mawunmi. She was pregnant within a month of meeting Bolaji. At just twenty-two, barely three years older than Bolanle who by now was in University of Lagos studying Economics and seven years older than Deoye, who was excelling well in secondary school.

Bolaji intended to keep the whole affair quiet and marry his young second wife on the down low. There were no hitches from local law regarding polygamy not in Ondo town but the grapevine and gossip spreaders did their work and the rumours reached Lagos.

Abeke heard the gist through various sources and though she didn't want to dismiss the rumour wanted concrete evidence. However when word came through a reliable source in family friend Mrs Somefun, (pronounced shom-eh-foon), Tayo and Funmi's mother, she knew there was substance to the word that was going around. Abeke decided to confront her husband about his extra marital activity and how he intended accommodating his latest offspring. Though she didn't hold any grudges against an unborn child, neither did she entertain the thought of bringing some young bush girl into her household with her rural ways and juju (black magic) concoctions. This wasn't an option at all.

She was only too aware of some disaster stories where first wives had been ejected from homes they had made by a combination of factors. Short sighted selfish husbands, juju having its way, and the wives themselves not being assertive enough, amongst other reasons. Abeke came straight up and confronted her husband. He admitted the truth and tried to justify everything by saying that it was his wifes outgoing nature that lead him to seek another woman, never being at home and often travelling here and there to pursue business interests. He wanted a wife he shouted, to be at home for him when he got home and be satisfied with what he provided for his family.

Bolaji was so far out of touch he didn't realise how much his wife had been contributing monetarily to their children's upbringing. She didn't flaunt it or beat her chest about it no documented evidence or records of what she had given, but her strife and love had been clearly evident and left an impression forever etched on her children's heart.

Bolaji wed his young concubine in Ondo town his home town it was a much celebrated affair with all his siblings and blood relatives present , though his wife and children did not attend. All refused point blank. Disappointed with her father Bolanle stayed in University with her friends and Deoye stayed at his friends Tayo Somefun house. They broke down the gist. Deoye sought the male support and solace so crucial at the sensitive age of fifteen plus. Between them that night, they both pledged to treat their prospective spouses with the greatest respect and devotion.

"You'd better do just that my man, cos I know you got your eye on my sister Funmi" Tayo teased.

Abeke needed no excuse for her not attending the masquerade of her husband's second wedding. Knowing her children were safely occupied for the weekend she stayed at her sisters deriving, spiritual,support and sisterly love that can flow so deep.

Where did she go from here? Her husband taking a second wife didn't represent any love lost, as long ago that part of their marriage had been dormant but at forty-six she still knew she had a lot of life to live. She forgave her husband but could no longer stay in the same house as him and rented a modest flat in Bagada, a relatively new estate in Lagos.

With the proceeds from her now flourishing business she could comfortably put down the years advance rent and cover the monthly rent while continuing to provide for her two children regardless of what her husband contributed towards them. Deoye was happy with the situation. He felt that his parents had long since been divorced while living in the same household. If his mother was always going to be made to feel distant it was best she was distant, rather than enduring the mental and physical torment she had for so long.

Abeke contrived to be as rounded as possible despite her husbands obvious and consistent efforts to kill her spirit and shackle his wife.

"You can take the man out of the bush but not the bush out of the man" Abeke would say to her son when he expressed his displeasure. Deoye agreed.

Bolanle was more hurt by her parents split, though she had strong suspicions that her father might be even more aggressive towards her mother as the shouting and threats from her father that she witnessed whenever she was home from university. It all seemed excessively violent but Bolaji took care not to actually get physical on his wife whenever his daughter was around between semesters. On many occasion Bolanle would find her mother crying and on enquiring what the problem was she would be told it was menopause or a migraine. Anything to throw her off scent as Abeke intended to protect her daughter from the truth in her usual self sacrificing way. Deoye would play dumb too. Whenever his sister asked

"What's up with mom?" He would front immaturity and pretend he hadn't noticed anything different from his mothers usual buoyant nature. Though he would always let her know of his sisters concern and again and again emphasise that his mom should save herself and leave her husband. Deoye knew his mother had the financial independence as he sometimes helped her out with basic administrative duties using the fundamental accountancy skill his father had drummed into his head on many a unwelcome midnight tutorial. He saw the figures involved and knew his mother was doing just fine.

Besides, by now whenever Bolaji's temper became rowdy Deoye would come and stand guard just to see that things stayed on the verbal plane only. And the times when things spilt over to as much as his father holding his mother, Deoye would step in and free his fathers grasp most times at the expense of his dad shifting the focus of his physical exertion to his son. These were really brutal episodes Bolaji would only stop when he became tired. Which when you are in your late forties, cholesterol lining your blood vessels from years of rich Nigerian food and a round barrel beer belly to match, meant two or three minutes tops. For the whole duration of the beating Deoye would cover up Ali style and not say a thing. While his mother would say "Don't hit him back Adeoye pele, pele." When his dad had punched himself out he would stand their panting and begin cursing his son omoale! omoale! Until he walked off leaving the house cursing.

The split was best for all. No legal wranglings Abeke just quietly left. She felt rid of a great burden and began to feel liberated again. Her children would come to see her and Bolanle would only stay at her mothers place. Deoye though, understood why he reluctantly had to stay with his dad after his mothers admonishment. He was overjoyed for his mother and on the occasions that she would visit her son and estranged husband communication was cordial but functional. Bolaji would not concede that he had lost a good woman to anyone but in his heart deep down he knew the truth. He would compensate himself with his now weekly trips to Ondo to see his iyawo. And come back fooling himself and trying to convince everyone on his return that his Mawunmi could prepare any food that Abeke could just as well with interest. No one was deceived.

It was Abekes maternal instinct that indirectly lead to her death. Just after her stepsons first birthday, which Bolaji had marked with an elaborate celebration in Ondo. Abeke had prepared to take a solo drive to see the infant and do her part as the senior wife.

She shopped for a good week in down town Lagos buying imported clothes food stuffs medicines and other infant accessories. Abeke addressed her children and explained why she was making the day trip. As she anticipated what objections her children would put forward. Abeke knew she had to make this journey she had resolved this and confided in Mrs Somefun, her long time friend about her intentions who had also advised her to take Deoye with her but Abeke knowing her son, had decided to go alone. This trip was a diplomatic venture and Deoye would just be squeezing face all the time and hardly acknowledge his fathers side of the family, multiple cousins and all which would only be taken as it was meant . . . unveiled dislike for his petty scheming relatives.

While he had inherited his mothers prowess in conversation he was as blunt as a spade and coupled with his fathers stubbornness Deoye more often than not came across as too assertive, which was often seen as threatening. Such misconceptions didn't have a place on this journey. Deoye had to stay behind.

"Why can't I make the trip and drop the stuff off with a letter ma? I don't want you going up there for anything you know how these people will look for any opportunity to do anything with their juju and things. They go open teeth for your front but plan wicked thing for your back." Deoye objected in reference to his now super bias opinion of his fathers family using fluent pigeon English.

"Adeoye, Adeoye! These are your fathers people so they are part of you accept that and control and channel your anger to good use. Forgive and move on. That is why I have to go. I need to manifest that the God I serve is bigger than any malicious thoughts and I wont let the devil have his way." Abeke explained.

She felt for her son and understood his anger but hoped maturity would help him to harness his thoughts and passion.

Bolanle understood that her mother was doing the right thing by making this trip even though her heart didn't agree with the idea of her mother travelling some two hundred kilometres alone she knew tradition and her mothers high regard for social tact would prevail.

"I understand why you have to go ma but let me go with you please ma?" Bolanle pleaded.

"Omo mi (My child). Don't worry, I'll be fine I need to go alone but God's with me." Abeke's words belied what she knew, justified genuine concern for their mother was being voiced. They were too aware of the master plan from Ondo. Which was to eliminate both mother and children and move in the home grown Mawunmi with their favourite son Bolaji. She had to protect her children from any such plot. She knew how to play her in-laws. She was going to do the right thing Abeke had found peace through Christianity. She was filled with the Holy Spirit and had prayed hard before deciding to embark on this journey. She travelled alone . . . and died alone.

While negotiating the road between Ore and Ondo, a forty kilometre stretch of winding road where motorist daringly overtook one another on corners with no respect for the dual carriage. The road was barely wide enough to take two vehicles, one in either direction let alone when it demanded three on the road whenever over taking occurred. Abeke was the one fatal victim of such a scenario.

While cautiously taking her Peugeot 505 around a sharp corner she was confronted by a truck carrying timber, trying to over take another truck carrying livestock. Both travelling at around 100km/ph far over the limit. Abeke swerved the car trying to avoid the inevitable but the last thing she saw in her 46 years of life was the two drivers smiles as they had obviously been competing, turn to surprise as both ploughed into the 505 passenger side at top speed pushing the car 70 metres as they struggled with their faulty hydraulic brakes to come to a halt. Her last sight was of these two drivers, her last thoughts were God be with my children.

Abeke was buried in Lagos as her brothers and sister took care of the whole event and angrily blamed Bolaji for their sisters death. Bolaji couldn't really offer much of an objection to the arrangement he was present with some of his blood relatives and genuinely grieved at the loss of his first wife but pride kept him from openly admitting it had been indirectly his fault.

His children refused to talk to him. Bolanle needed solitude, Deoye was more vocal and eventually caused his father to relocate to Ondo to seek solace around his people, new wife and child. In whose eyes he could do no wrong. That is what he needed and thrived on, the massaging of his unstable ego by receiving the psychological masturbation that made him feel good, feel he was a man, feel he was the man. Bolaji Olaiya couldn't hang in London where his culture and colour was undermined and threatened. Or Lagos, where the fast competitive life style didn't suit him either. In Ondo the tempo was slower and predominantly rural it suited his nature, there he was the man, the local champion. No questions of his manhood no having to change to fit in, that was home, where his heart was.

Over the next four years Bolajis relationship with his children deteriorated. He had never kept them close, never knew how. As his father before him, he never understood the need to communicate with them. That was been Abekes forte but now she was gone.

Bolanle lived in denial for some months but eventually found it within herself to forgive her father for his part in bringing about her mothers death. With no positive inspiration from her parents marriage, Bolanle was disillusioned with men and avoided them with chronic suspicion. She had no intentions of marrying young and immersed herself into Christianity as her mother had done nurturing her spirit to deal with the pain of her grief. The only male she gave time to was her brother Deoye she hoped he would pull through and that the contempt he had for his father would pass. She applied herself to her university degree and kicked second class upper honours. Then she set about building up her professional resume working first in the finance ministry, then in the private sector for a multi-national pharmaceutical company. She was on her way to making herself an independent woman as her mother had done.

Independence was what Deoye was struggling with. His Father had heavy handedly tried to dictate every thing in his life. Deoye succumbed while his mother was alive. She was his chill factor.

He held no reservations in blaming his father for her death. But still lived with his father who returned to Lagos on admonishment from his moms brothers and sister to try and keep a semblance of a family. But it was Abeke Olaiya who had kept any hope of that family being. Deoye missed her guiding hand in his boy-to-man phase and wondered what had made his father the way that he was. They were strangers in the same house with little communication.

Deoye would sit in his room listening to music, BBC world service or watching CNN when he wasn't studying. Inspired by the way the presenters and sports commentators painted vivid pictures with the use of the English language, he decided he wanted to pursue a career in the media. However his father refused to pay for his university education unless he studied Accountancy, Law or another more socially recognised professional degree.

Deoye made up his mind to come back to England and chase his dream. He decided to pursue his career in London and confront a different type of oppression. A subtle, racially bias and ignorant oppression that had tormented and frustrated his Fathers mind years before. He was ready to take his chances and began to hustle the money for his one way ticket. However his dual culture wreaked havoc with his spirit. Though all his hardships had precipitated a wealth of cultural identity, he couldn't make his home in Nigeria. His mother was gone and there was no father-son bond to break. Once Deoye told his father his intentions he was against the idea and refused to give Deoye his blessings or even speak to him unless his son fell in line. Further more, Bolaji refused to give his son any financial help saying he'd end up doing menial manual labour unless he stayed in Nigeria and studied.

There was no love lost between father and son when Deoye at twenty, returned independently to England. Initially he felt free of his fathers manipulative, controlling presence, though he missed the community spirit of Lagos. The paradox was compounded when he realised and was made to realise how Nigerian he was. Though he wasn't as thorough bred as his father, he began to understand how his father had been frustrated starting from scratch as a young man from Nigeria in London

Chapter One

"Damn I need to sort it?" Deoye said to himself, his thoughts continued.

Here's me, Twenty two. 'Been back in this country now eighteen months or so. What have I achieved? I still can't get a grant, I' got three A/levels from Nigeria, a C.A.M. (Communication Advertising and Marketing) certificate from here and a first year completed in a Media Studies diploma. That and self belief is all I got going for me."

On the outside looking in, I am just a bum. I ain't shit! Who wants to give a black man a chance? A Black Man! Not merely a brain washed, ethnic minority classed, Black British male. A real Black Man that wants to express himself in a place of work without selling out. All of his culture, his upbringing, his morality, tenacity, creativity, passion, self confidence, his pepper eating, shorts drinking, circumcised dick and all. Then harness all these attributes to the needs of a corporate establishment. Who would accept such a Black man and provide genuine prospects of climbing the corporate ladder in whatever capacity"?"

"Why do so many of the Black guys here seem to wear their colour as a façade, just on the exterior with no depth? Otherwise they willingly don't delve into or deny their rich black culture to find out or recognise who they are? I'm not gonna hide who I am like a bad birth mark. I' sure spent nuff time finding out. I want you to see my black arse coming at ya. It ain't all good but what culture is? Why should I accept just being tolerated as some ethnic minority quota? I want to be understood, appreciated and accepted being myself ." Deoye stressed again in his mind.

"I'll make it being me here". Deoye told himself. "If there's no space for me, I'll make myself some damn space. I ain't goin' down like my Pop, frustrated and bitter. I will make it! Right now Black man you'd better keep it real and keep hustling, cuz you've got a signing on gig to catch."

Two minutes past three, he was running late but the queue there would probably be still building up. The usual faces, of which he felt ashamed to be part of, would all be there. Deoye selected his casual beige jacket from the wardrobe and shuffled it on while kicking his beaten Nike sneakers from under the bed. He sat down on the bed, pulled on his footwear and tucked the laces into the basket ball boots between the worn lining and his socks. Standing up and walking towards his room door shoved the loose change into his jeans pocket. He opened his bedroom door as wide as it would go, being limited by the wardrobe behind the door, and slid his frame through the tight space in the doorway. Dragging the door shut he noticed the thread bare bedroom carpet and locked his room door.

"I gotta get out of this joint". He declared out loud, jumping down the stairs of the three bedroom semi. He paused to take the head phones of his walkman, which was ever present in the jacket, from the pocket and fixed them on his head while looking down at the second post on the door mat. Three items;

One readers digest prize draw invitation to Miss Victoria Kaye, a reminder letter for his overdue catalogue payment and what was probably a new credit card for John Fuller, the third co-tenant. John was O.K., from a working class family in South London. A graduate in history now working as a civil servant in Central London somewhere. Victoria, twenty four, came from a middle class background. She had only recently come to live in London but had relatively little interactive experience with black people. Both her parents were medical doctors up in the West country, where she frequently visited on the many holidays she enjoyed as a primary school teacher.

Deoye felt sorry for the youth of today. And wondered how someone quite so ignorant of the cultural diversity expressed in today's classrooms could possibly give a rounded and well balanced foundation for education. The worse thing was that she was not aware that she needed to enhance her cultural awareness not just in the interest of her professional pursuits but for the cause of a greater understanding in the world today for a better tomorrow. Victoria was a victim of her upbringing.

Deoye was happy to put her straight at every opportunity whenever she made judgments based on those stereotypical idiosyncrasies and he was learning to do so with a softly softly approach, despite how off base and fundamentally naive and stupid the comments often were.

Deoye opened the front door and stepped outside. As he slipped his hand inside the jacket pocket to press the play button on his personal stereo. He could feel the familiar rigid hexagonal shape of a fifty pence piece. Drawing the coin out to confirm between his first and index fingers he smiled to himself and began singing as he slammed the door shut and broke into a jog . . .

"The blacker the berry the sweeter the juice . . . " Deoye sang along with the Alfonso Hunter jam as the heavy bass line pounded loud in the earphones. Deoye lengthened his stride and turned out of his road into Colindale Avenue. Stepping up his pace he crossed a junction and sped into the station. Momentarily checking his stride to observe whether there were any inspectors at the barrier. No guards,

"It's all good." Deoye thought as he heard tube doors opening on the Southbound platform.

Stepping up his stride Deoye reached the top of the stairs and turned right. Bad choice, his route to the train was barred by a young black mother at the bottom of the stairs struggling to fold a pushchair and hold an infant while his toddler brother was scurrying up the stairs counting.

". . . Fwee . . . Four . . . Five ."

"Careful Trey!" His mother called from the bottom of the stairs. Deoye thought quickly.

"Come on Trey!" He said taking one long stride over six steps to pick up the toddler.

"Cute" he thought as he swirled the child around and put him down at the top of the stairs then turned to fly back down them again. Trey giggled at the thrill of being carried at speed and this made Deoye break out a smile. Reaching the bottom of the stairs Deoye paused to consider helping the young mother.

"Do you need a hand?" Deoye offered the young mother.

She had succeeded in collapsing the baby buggy and baby bag on one shoulder, infant in left hand. She dexterously managed to scoop up the buggy in the right hand and begin climbing the stairs.

"Nah I'm alright." She uttered without so much as a side ways look at Deoye who stood appreciating just how alright she did look. In a composed and a physically appealing way despite managing with two sub three year old kids. Deoye attempted to decipher the young mothers response.Maybe her refusal to accept a genuine offer of chivilary was borne from a bad experience with a man or maybe different men. Another irresponsible father perhaps who had made a young sister pregnant and just missed off the scene. It had happened too often now girlfriend had acquired a subconscious barrier to any male interest what so ever. Regardless of the level of interest or how well mannered the approach may be. That scenario had been played out but maybe he was wrong he conceded. By default part of him always wanted to reach out to such a sister and show them a little TLC. Let them know that there is hope a Black man can deliver.

"Cool!" Deoye turned to see a now diminishing gap between the tube doors. Trey , who was still giggling at the top of the stairs, began calling,

"Daddy! daddy!" And Deoye could see out of the corner of his eye that he was pointing to him with an out stretched chubby first finger. Deoye let a little smile bust loose as he observed Trey's mother once more adding weight to his theory of her domestic situation and that she was all right from behind too. With barely an eighteen inch gap between the doors, he managed to board the train side ways before the doors closed. His momentum threw him hard against the opposite doors.

Straightening himself up, Deoye adjusted his dislodged earphones and brought his Walkman out of his pocket. He had somehow managed to depress the stop button during his unconventional entrance.

Engrossed in checking the working order of his walkman Deoye took a seat as the train started to move out of the station. Having been focused head down, he noticed a pair of well manicured feet, wearing easy open toed sandals. The nails were painted, beige flawlessly applied and the skin pleasingly seemed naturally tanned. Without looking up Deoye assumed she was possibly Jewish maybe,Italian or Greek, size six feet, he concluded and resumed his appreciation of the girls fine legs which were clad in a pair of fitted paisley jacquard hipsters.

Aware of the attention she was receiving the girl recrossed her legs. Deoye let out a long gust of air. She caught him and smirked as she peered over her rimless glasses, pouted, blinked and then met Deoye's full gaze. They looked at each other square for a good five seconds. Deoye took in her looks.

"Gotta be Southern European, uh huh. Square jaw line and full lips that were saying mmmmmaah! Eye brows broad and thick looking like the Puma sports wear logo above each dark eye bordered with equally thick and long eye lashes. Mmmm. Classy babe" he concluded. Now satisfied his walkman was alright. Deoye removed his earphones and broke the ice .

"Hi"

"Hello" came the reply "Did you hurt yourself when you got on the train?" Deoye thought about lying and faking a dislocation of the shoulder.

"Nah I'm O.K. I was thinking my stereo might be busted but it's fine. Same word I might have used to describe you on first impressions. If you don't mind my observation. How are you doin?"

"I'm fine" Taking Deoye's subtle compliment in her stride, the girl seemed to open up. "What were you listening to?"

"Aah some easy mid-tempo stuff. Alphonso Hunter . . . The blac . . .

"The players anthem, The Way Players Play, right?" The girl anticipated while lowering her Marie Claire magazine and recrossing those fit legs again.

"No, no" Deoye replied trying to dislodge any thoughts the girl may have formed that he was a player "Have you heard the whole album?"

"Can't say I have but I like his voice"

"O.K. I got a little sumthin, sumthin for ya" Deoye cued the track he had in mind, trying to drop a little innuendo as he worked smoothly through nought to sixty on this fine girl. The opening base line pumped. "Here you go" Deoye offered the earphones. The girl raised one eyebrow, she looked even cuter. But Deoye understood her reservations based on personal hygiene.

"Oh I'm sorry. Please don't be offended, but this brother's real clean. No wax deposits in these ears." Deoye didn't miss the opportunity to pose his profile and move closer so that the girl could inspect his ears. She gave a light ripple of laughter and allowed herself a slight smile. She had clocked Deoyes favourite feature and moved forward bending her head to allow him to place the phones in her ears.

Again their eyes met, fixed as Deoye pushed her short rich hair back to expose her ears. She steadied his hands as he placed the mini speakers. He could feel her soft breath and smell her Monsoon perfume. Their faces were no more than six inches apart. Trying to keep his gaze on her face he struggled to keep his eyes from looking directly at her cleavage, which he had already clocked as 36C. Still gazing at the flawless lipstick on the pout Deoye began to imitate the bass line.

"Check the lyrics" he said as Alphonso's voiced cut in . . .

"The blacker the berry, the sweeter the juice . . . . . ."

Girl took it all in and blushed as her cover was blown, she played right into his hands Deoye thought as he cruised on forty-five. Babe moved back in her seat and began to gather her things to alight.

"The blacker the berry the sweeter the juice! So what do you think?" Deoye asked congratulating himself on his handling of the face off.

"Are you talking about his voice, or that particular opinion?" Deoye sat forward again. "You already told me you like his voice" Deoye eliminated in a deep, mellow ,smoothed out voice, now raising his eyebrows.

Recomposed girl friend returned the gaze and matter of factly replied.

"I wouldn't know. I have no experience from which to offer an opinion." Light was now appearing at the end of the tunnel, metaphorically, as Deoye saw the reply as overt encouragement to offer an opportunity to create a situation where blackberry juice might be sampled. Also literally, as the train emerged from the tunnel and begun to decelerate pulling into Hendon Central station. Deoye took the answer as a green light. As the girl rummaged through her bag and stood up he was about to resume pressure on the accelerator, when just behind him came the voice of ultimate kill joy.

"Tickets please!"

Observing as the object of his attention brought out a gold card with a black and white mug shot cut in a perfect square, same pout, same glasses some how looking even sexier, she held up the zone three and zone four annual gold card for the ticket inspector to see.

"Thank you" the inspector said flashing a mechanical smile as he averted his attention to Deoye. "Tickets please."

Deoye felt his armpit start itching and his heart beat fluttering as he watched babe look straight at him and obviously deduce from the sorry look on his face, that he didn't have a ticket or a pass. She appeared disappointed as she stood up and moved towards the double door exit with her head down. The tube gradually came to a halt.

The inspector by now had also read the signs and manouvered himself into a position to prevent any hurried escape plans the fare avoider may have been cooking up.

Deoye was focusing on the babes butt in the hipsters, tight on the end of those legs and as she stood waiting for the doors to open her profile told the tail had definition.

"No VPL too, that must be a thong she's wearing." His thoughts were interrupted by the inspectors persistence in verifying whether his suspect had paid his tariff .

"Do you have a ticket?" Deoye thought of making a run for it. But dismissed the idea concluding how void of sang - froid such a move would have been.

"Erm yeah, I er had to rush at Colindale to get the train, see I was supposed to sign on at 3.00p.m. I'm er running late." Deoyes voice had taken over the silence left by the train finally coming to a halt. His excuse violently demolished any self esteem he was attempting to preserve. In retrospect, doing a runner would have been the better option. The train doors opened. "Shhhhummpp!"

Punctuating Deoyes pathetic excuse. Everybody in the carriage seemed to direct their gaze at him before departing from the train. Once more his eyes met the girl he had been working on. She parted her lips slightly and raised her right puma eye brow again giving Deoye that disappointed look which escalated his embarrassment.

"You are aware that you're obliged to have a valid ticket before you start your journey?" The inspector was now convinced Deoye hadn't paid for his journey and without the power to detain offending passengers made movements towards the door as Deoye was making moves to alight while pulling the lose coins out of his pocket .

"Here you go, I got the fare." He offered the pile to the inspector as they both stepped out onto the platform.The inspector offered his right hand for the change and signaled to the driver at the front end of the tube to wait, while he collected the outstanding fare.

Deoye pulled out his signing on UB40 leaflet to reach the prize 50p piece.

"See! I did mean to pay even though times are real hard as you can see. It's all there and then some boss." Deoye said, slapping his income support book in his palm while the inspector counted out the assortment of coppers and five pence pieces, periodically pausing to shuffle piles of coins to the value of ten pence into the left hand and emphasise a point while stressing the ramifications of being caught without a ticket for the whole journey.

"I'll let you off this time. Next time you may not be so lucky"

"Hey thanks." Deoye took off on the platform only to be called back by the inspector for his receipt. Murmuring his thanks again he ran off up the platform hoping to catch another glance at that thonged butt. He jumped up the stairs of Hendon Central station. No joy.

"I guess with legs like that she would be making long strides" he thought disappointed.

He was a little late, but Deoye hated queuing so hopefully the crowd would have subsided, he passed through the subway under Watford Way and acknowledged the busker that was always present whenever he passed through to sign on, which had been over two months now. Deoye felt a twinge of guilt as he usually dropped some loose change for the wanna be Noel Gallagher, but this time, as Noel strummed Wonderwall there was no familiar cling of loose change landing in the guitar case. Just a mutual understanding of hard times as they both looked at each other with a don't-let-the-bastards-grind-you-down nod.

The Employment Office was fairly crowded. Deoye recognised some of the regulars and they did likewise greeting him, or giving the same nod that had been exchanged with Noel in the subway. He took a ticket from the dispenser, number 64. The L.E.D. display over head showed number 57.

BING! the number changed to 58. Five more numbers before his came up. He sat parallel to the window just under the number display unit and surveyed the normal melee that was common place in the signing on office.

At an administrators desk a young Somalian guy was being talk ed down to by an administration assistant with a loud local accent, while trying to register a new claim for income support.

"You mean you've come here without a pen and you want to sign on. Fill this and all the parts marked with an X and make sure I get the pen back, I've lost enough pens today."

"Hmmmphh" Deoye reflected, "As if my man had been stealing the pens one by one." His attention was caught, as was most people in the office, by a claimant in the office who was clearly pissed off about something.

"What do you mean it'll be another week,? it's been six effing weeks already" every bloody week you piss me about here. What am I suppose to live on?"

"There's no need to swear Mr Carr, but you didn't sign on two weeks ago when you were suppose to."

"I called the office and told you I had a days packing job in Wembley"

"You never spoke to me Mr Carr and its not recorded on your file" The mechanical bureaucrat defended the system.

"Then that's another cock up you've made then!" Mr Carr was spitting with rage.

"I'm afraid you'll have to make a new claim. Please take a form and a ticket and see the lady at the desk over there."

"Sod new claim I want my money now !!!" 59 and 60 flashed by in quick succession as Mr Carr mumbled something derogatory about the social security system and the government in general.

"Could you go and wait in Room 3 Mr Carr, I'll get some one to see you in private."

"He better have my bloody cheque."

Number 61 came up as Deoye watched a white N reg 5 series BMW pull up outside. Though his vision was partially obscured by a notice board in the room . He was sure he recognised the driver from back in Nigeria. The driver got out of the car. He could only make out the clothes the big guy was wearing.

Typically Nigerian. Armani jeans and a Ralph Lauren Oxford cotton shirt. The chap had a signing on leaflet in his hand, not your typical bonafide claimant. Deoye leaned forward and looked over his shoulder waiting for the doors to open. Another couple of white guys came in, talking about Arsenals prospects of getting into the Champions league as runners up while stubbing out their cigarettes then a pause. Deoye looked at the smooth white car outside again thinking the driver may have returned there then swang his eyes back to the door as the Beamer driver stepped in.

Though he had put on much weight Afolabi Shokoya still had the same arrogant strut he had exhibited since he was in secondary school. Deoye flashed back again.

After the Olaiyas reached Nigeria in 1984, Bolanle was registered in International School Ibadan. A very prestigious school in the south western Yoruba state of Oyo. The school in fact was sited in the grounds of University Of Ibadan Africa's first University. The students of I.S.I. were mostly indigines of Nigeria but there were many mixed race students and foreign students whose parents were ex-patriots, living in Nigeria with varied occupations. Lecturers, Contractors, Civil engineers whose lifestyles suited having there children in what was seen as an elite boarding school.

Meanwhile Deoye was sent to a school of hard knocks in Lagos state, Igbobi college in the heart of Lagos mainland. An all boys school full of streetwise adolescents. Lagos school life was always competitive from the classroom to the playground in that order of importance. It wasn't enough to achieve good grades alone you had to back that up with some street cred as well to preserve your own self esteem.

Afolabi Shokoya was the guru in street life and Deoye was the new boy from away with an attitude he stood out from most of the other first year students not just because of his strong North West london accent but more for his build being schooled Deoye with a years hard baptism in the school when he first got off the boat from England . Deoye was significantly bigger than most of his class mates despite being a year younger. As custom prevailed his seniors would impose their traditional reign of terror upon the boisterous or innocent juniors. One such senior, Solomon Lawal, interpreted Deoyes size and attitude as challenging and decided to test him with physical assignments.

After Deoyes hands had been blistered by completing Solomons instructed task of cutting the grass in the school playing field with a cutlass, his physical fitness was to be tested again when the same senior told him to do fifty press ups to flex some authority.

Keeping cool Deoyes face was contorted believing he could kick the seniors ass if he was back in London but in Nigeria, respect your seniors or else, was always threatened. He fought against every instinct to kiss his teeth and walk out of the classroom and went prostrate to perform the exercise.

Despite the grit and dirt burrowing into the open and burst blisters Deoye flowed to forty two push ups then had the punishment heightened by having one of the viewing seniors siting on his back. Deoye held in the up position his hands trembled from the added weight.

"What are you waiting for Olaiya I said fifty come on !" Lawal, the self appointed task master took out his belt and began flogging Deoye.

That was the breaking point at which instincts took over. He had learnt to cope with having to wear the school uniform, khaki shorts and shirt that were so stiff and uncomfortable compared to the smart slacks and blazer he had looked forward to wearing in North West London. He had adapted to having to play ing bare footed with a leather football. He had learnt to cope without so many things that he had become used to in London, but he couldn't accept being bullied. Deoye stood up throwing his jockey onto the floor.

"Ah Olaiya, O fe daran?" (Are you looking for trouble) Get down and give me another fifty jo!" Deoye stood with his hands folded in defiance and his posture giving his fresh North London attitude. Senior Solo slapped Deoye open handedly, tscchhh!

Before his hand had completed its momentum from his strike, he felt lower lip being smashed against his upper incisors and the taste of his own blood in his mouth. As his head reeled back Deoye resumed his stance only to be descended upon by three seniors beating him from all angles. Solo had by now recovered his poise and sought his vengeance for the humiliation bestowed upon him by this junior. His bottom lip was triple size and pulsating.

"Hmmph. Today, today Olaiya I will show you that I am a Lagos boy!"

The seniors held Deoye while Solo laced him two open handed slaps. After a third slap more insulting than injuring Deoye let loose with a kick to Solos groin.

"Yeeaaaay". Solo doubled over in pain. His cronies laid into the stubborn junior as he backed into a corner and covered up. As the beatings were beginning to take their toll on Deoye, Afolabi Shokoya stepped in.

"O fe pa omo e?"(Do you want to kill the boy)

Himself a notorious exponent of seniority punishment Shoko, as he was known, was hard sometimes excessively so on offending juniors, testing them with creative punishment but he somehow never laid his hands on anyone. He was in the forth year of secondary school fifteen, a year ahead of Solomon and his boys and pulled the seniority factor in calling them off of Deoye.

After hearing different versions of what lead to the fracas, he examined Deoye. whose face was puffy from the beating and uniform torn at the collar . Shokoya decided that the boy had served enough punishment and would probably get a further beating trying to explain to his parents his torn khaki once he got home.

Shokoya gave the group of third year students a brief lecture on the art of controlled aggression and looked at Deoye once more.

"Olaiya come and see me at break time tomorrow you hear?" Deoye nodded and was dismissed. Shokoya was well respected in the school left the classroom hailed by the third year students.

"Man Shokooo!" Though an aggrieved Solomon Lawal didn't offer any praise for his senior. He still wanted to inflict more pain on Deoye to avenge his aching groin and bust lip. As from that day Senior Solo was known as Senior-Ete (lip) which juniors had learnt to say quickly hence disguise to sound like seniority. A lasting legacy of the episode as his credibility as a disciplinarian was quashed.

Deoye showed up the next day with his best friend Tayo Somefun at Shokoya's classroom. Shoko genuinely liked the mature first year student and his close friend. The two of them had been well talked about as skillful footballer's in their year, but because of their sizes were often perceived as arrogant, by the likes of Solomon Lawal. Shokoya was a popular, pupil who sought the finer trimmings of life beyond what Nigeria had to offer. Born and raised in Nigeria. He was constantly dreaming and scheming a way out of the country and he saw Deoye with his British passport and Tayo whose father was a diplomat, as useful connections to have.

From the time Shokoya saved Deoye from his first encounter with his oppressive seniors, he struck up a good friendship with him. Shokoya was hustling him which was mutually O.K. as he derived protection from the friendship. Shoko would pick Deoyes brains on the way of life in England and learnt the diction and subtle mannerisms from his younger friend and the many other friends from away that he had acquired. They all served to add to Afolabi Shokoya's goal of total assimilation in the western world preferably State side or England and be free from the limitations of the cursed Nigerian green passport. Evidently he had made it.

"Shokoooo!" Deoye called out, standing up to embrace his bigger and older friend.

"Ah Olaiya, looong time!" Shokoya reservedly returned the greeting while plucking ticket number sixty nine from the dispenser. They gave each other the familiar Nigerian hand shake; the double clasp followed by a routine click with both index finger and thumb. "How far?" Shoko asked.

At six feet four inches tall and sixteen stone he now had the physical presence to go with the arrogance that had been present since he was a slightly tubby youth. But now he was solidly built it wasn't all fat. He worked weights and still played basketball as a mean power forward. Whenever he played he was referred to as Shak-O as he borrowed the style of the L.A. Lakers superstar while wearing an Orlando Magic 32 vest. He curiously gave his former school mate a once over looking for signs of good living.

"Man me, I just dey hustle."

Deoye replied in pigeon English, feeling his old friends assessment as Shoko's eyes paused on his plastic watch strap after the prolonged hand shake, not the sign of good living. He had heard on the grapevine that his old senior had been working the benefits system, having moved on from big time credit card fraud since he came over to England on a students visa in Autumn '91. Staying ahead of the system with many aliases. Word was that Shoko had a contract marriage arranged to legalise his stay as soon as he got into England. Shereese, a fine West Indian girl was the beneficiary of a rumoured £2500 for the deal. Shoko had tried to keep the cinnamon honey sweet over the years with the odd pressie of Chanel, cash or weekend in Paris while he got his things on occasion. However the situation was more complex now that Calvin who "hated Afikans especially Nigerians", Shereese's baby father was putting pressure on his baby mother to squeeze Shoko for more to feed his drugs game.

"You're looking good and things must be on the up. I don't mind that Beamer Shoko" Deoye commented.

"To know your way no be sin" came the casual acceptance of acknowledgment for the status symbol. "Shey na Mr Smith you be here or which one? " Shoko was seeking whether Deoye was onto Odu (fraudulent deal) or his attending the job centre was as that of a loser with no resource of his own imagination or motivation, a waste of British passport.

"No Shoko. You know me I come straight. I'm taking a year out of college to raise funds. It's not easy shuffling work plus school, landlord go take his own . . ."

"Tax man go take his own, council tax go come again , phone bill no go tell you say it's good to talk . . . I know the deal my guy." Shokoya completed the typical daily, weekly and monthly demands on the pay cheque that were so familiar to young independent guys trying to find their feet without the stability of a parents house and home to lessen the burden.

"But like I said to know your way no be sin." Repeated Shoko as number 62 flashed up to attend counter three." So what's your plan my man, Cos you said you want to be like eh, Garth Crooks abi?" Shokoya made a sarcastic reference to Deoye's long term intent to channel his communicative attributes into sports media, in ever fluent pigeon english. He saw the remark hurt his friend maybe more that it was meant to.

"How is Somefun do you hear from him? I hear he's scattering things in Amsterdam on the field and off."

Deoye was well proud of the fact that Tayo Somefun, his childhood friend, had kept his focus and ambition alive and arrived in the world of professional football. The two friends had both been selected for the Nigerias youth football team "The Green Eaglets"; Arguably the best under 17 talent in the world of football in both 1989 and 1991. Though Deoyes father blocked his sons participation. Claiming that his son would miss out on valuable academic time and seized his passport. Tayo made the squad in both selections. His father as a diplomat, couldn't and wouldn't make the kind of statement that his friends father had done. He was relatively spoilt by his father, so once he declared his intent to become a professional footballer, having manifested the natural talent and dedication his father gave his blessing.

Mr Somefun was often out of the country in an official capacity and was very proud of his sons potential and prospects in representing his country. In1989 when both were 15 Nigeria were eliminated in the quarter finals by eventual winners Saudi Arabia. Tayo never got to play in the tournament as a hamstring injury ruled him out. In 1991 Nigeria were banned from the competition by F.I.F.A. At seventeen this was his last chance to play for the Eaglets. He graduated to the Under 20s team catching the eye of many European scouts and was signed as an eighteen year old for top Dutch club Amsterdam F.C. as an outstanding attacking left sided midfielder.

He spent the next two years honing his skills and acquiring the nick name "Some Fun," the English pronunciation of his real name was given from his happy go lucky approach to his game and the perpetual smile, he seemed to have whenever he played, despite the close attention and rough treatment his ever growing reputation had brought from opposing defenders in the domestic and European matches. His critics cited that his love for the nightlife in Amsterdam was the sole reason for his nickname as he was often known to be up in the early hours of the morning clubbing in the red light districts of Holland's capital. This had brought about some recent disciplinary measures. He sat on the bench with the likes of Kanu as company throughout the 1994 world cup as Daniel Amocachi took the plaudits playing in his position and at 22 a lack of match fitness prevented him breaking into Nigerias gold medal winning 96 Olympic team. Yet he was not a first team regular with Amsterdam.

Rumour was the club wanted to offload him for at least four million pounds before the Bosman ruling prevented them getting a penny for their investment in nurturing his talent, at the end of the 1997/98 season when his five year contract was up.

"Yeah Tayo keeps in touch all the time in fact he came over last month with his club for the UEFA cup quarter-finals with Villa, sent me tickets too but I couldn't get up to Birmingham . . .Well for the very same reasons you see me signing on today"

"Ah the boy played well that night I beg ! He's arrived what about you Olaiya? So no coins to go see your right man play, just travel money oh! Are times that hard?" Shokoya was sincerely disappointed that Deoye didn't seem to be on the way up, not making the progress he had expected from him . . . legally or otherwise.

"Shoko nah small by small some of us no wan' odu now." Deoye felt offended by his old protector's presumption that he was slacking and content with his current status quo.

" Just say the word and I could school you, If you're still pally with Some Fun it's all good as pe this thing dey flow for Amsterdam beaucoup and you get british passport abi?" Shokoya dropped a hint towards his drug trafficking. Surprised Deoye responded.

"Eh Heh"

"Then whenever you're ready. Nah Britico like you I dey wait since to go-come, collect-drop. If say I had your number I for connect you . . ."

"Wait, wait, Shoko". Deoye dropped the pigeon English. "You've done what you wanna do, you're doin' what you wanna do. Big white Beamer, the Ralph, Armani, Gucci and" . . . Deoye paused to pull up his friends shirt sleeve looking for his watch. "You see and a Ramond Weil gold watch! "It ain't like I ain't got taste for all that shit . Yeah I want it all . All of that and then some all the trimmings, but at what price? What's the cost Shoko, Uh ? Freedom!" Deoye answered his own question. "As if Black Man hasn't been imprisoned or enslaved long enough already. Constantly looking over my shoulder, on the run? Uh Uh. I can't be a prisoner of my own conscience or anything for that matter other than my dreams and ambitions for the time being. I will make it my way doing what I wanna do."

Number 63 came up to punctuate Deoyes monologue. It took conscious effort to express the passion and annoyance he felt and keep his voice down to a deep forceful whisper.

"Hmmph Olaiya, Olaiya." Shokoya gathered his thoughts and flashed his arrogant smug smile. "You keep your idealistic bullshit Olaiya you've got your British passport . You didn't have a customs man stick his a surgical gloved finger up your arse when you got off the plane like I did"! Deoye winced at the thought. Shokoya continued.

"You mention conscience eh? Oyingbo (white people) get conscience for black mans arrested development? After helping themselves to the best of Africa for hundreds of years? Tschh"! Shokoya kissed his teeth. "I'm just making sure I have enough for my lifetime, plenty go remain, no guilt conscience." Shokoyas voice was just as expressive but significantely less flustered. He paused as the number register beeped again he pointed.

"64 Mr Olaiya your number's up, so hurry up and grasp your thin strand of reality , because Number 69 is me, Mr Collins, I'm waiting to get mine!" Shokoya held up his signing on leaflet close to Deoyes face to read his alias. "Yes number 69, I'm gonna fuck the Oyingbo's system every which way I can."

Deoye admired Shoko's conviction even if he didn't agree with his modus operandi in acquisition of the material things which he had always sought.

"Listen Mr Collins don't get a crick in that neck looking over that big shoulder O.K. I gotta go."

"Man me, I'm so busy looking in the mirror at how good I look, that I'll see whatever may be coming from behind if anything."

Again impressed by the self assured nature of the response, Deoye smiled and acknowledged his friend by offering his hand for that handshake again . . . click! He turned to attend the counter to perform the fortnightly ritual. Slipping the benefit leaflet under the glass divider the same assistant that was on the Somalian claimants case took it and made an attempt at pronouncing his surname.

"Oh-la-iyer?"

"Olaiya! Ola- Iya!" Deoye exaggerated the correct pronunciation with his best Yoruba dialect. It brought home Shokoyas harsh but fair analysis of British apathy. Having colonised countries all over the world and beating their chest about the Great British Empire, now the Commonwealth. It was the people who were around to witness that empire whom are the least receptive of the diverse cultures represented from the former colonies. On this occasion the ignorance was manifested by the poor attempt at his surname.

The assistant marked an X on a green slip for him to sign next to. Deoye scrawled the semblance of his name and turned to leave the office.

"Can I have the pen back please?" The assistant shouted.

Deoye felt small and mumured an apology as he put the pen back under the counter.

Turning once more to leave he bumped into an irate Mr Carr.

. . ." six effing weeks . . ! Ooops sorry mate, It's a bloody joke ain't it?" The bloody systems a mess ay ?"

"Yeah it's real' slack Boss." Deoye's eyes were searching for Shokoya as he made his way towards the exit. He noticed the big guy approaching the far counter and thought momentarily about hailing him. Nah let it go he thought. He could do without his sharp retort after his ego had just reached its lowest ebb. He had to get a job for his own self respect and to help fuel his dreams of a career in the media.

Coming out of the Signing on office Deoye turned left back towards the tube station walking slowly he slid his hands inside his jacket pocket, Feeling the control buttons on his walkman he shut out the temptation of playing some Alphonso Hunter.

" I gotta be a hustler now not a player Alphons, a hustler"! His head down he walked on, fumbling inside his jacket pocket he brought out his cash point card amidst an assortment of scrappy pieces of paper, a two week old lottery ticket, Kit-Kat wrapper, Vibe magazine subscription form and other scraps. He examined and discarded each piece individually and paused as he viewed the reverse side of the lottery ticket. Funmi Somefun 0181 202 9298.

He hadn't seen Funmi for three months. She had just moved into a three bedroom flat near Brent street, No more than a ten minute walk from the station, with two friends. This was conveniently close to the Middlesex University campus where she was studying a post graduate degree in European Languages. Deoye never hid the fact that he had a serious soft spot for Tayo's older sister. Though she was barely a year older than himself, she too had benefited from their fathers position as a Nigerian foreign diplomat. As she could mingle easily in the elite circles and cliques that privileged Nigerians in London gravitated to.

Despite all she had going for her, wealth famous footballing little brother and and all, she was a very smart and likeable person. A straight "A" student with a vibrant personality but she chose to be relatively understated which complimented her subtle good looks, Tall, dark and lovely with a distinct long neck and a packed size twelve frame. Deoye contemplated looking her up. His deliberations were disturbed by a car horn.

Afolabi Shokoya waved a hand from behind the wheel of his left hand drive Beamer, cruised by and turned right. Only now did Deoye notice the full number plate, N166A . Was that a reference to NIGGA? Either way the subtle use of the sixes was instrumental in the interpretation of the personalised plate. Shoko was making his statement. Pure player, living fast and large, Big Willie style.

"I'll get mine , for sure but I gotta hustle right now." His thoughts went back to Funmi. Just as he missed her brother Tayo he missed her too. She was special, no other girl not even his sister, seemed to vibe with him like Funmi. They could talk for hours she could hold her own on any topic and football was regularly the subject when her brother and Deoye were around. She was a real trooper. "Black coffee," he used to call her, no sugar, no cream. Dark, rich subtle taste and very stimulating, physically and mentally. He smiled recalling how she just called him D. The only flaw he found in her was her often expensive taste, and they were virtually cousins.

Reminiscing over when they were both teenagers growing up in Lagos, Deoye slowly played over in his mind times when they would cuddle up close no more than that in private. It seemed so long ago, but he sometimes wondered what would happen if they weren't practically family, cousins. Now her shit was so tight and he just had his scattered distant dreams. Things had to change, he vowed not to see her until he had something going on and he vowed to see her soon.

Chapter Two

Amane Al- Shifa swirled the keys to her flat around the well manicured index finger of her right hand as she approached home. Men! She thought . . . and boys too. The black guy she had met on the train seemed to have the rugged looks, confidence and spontaneous creativity that she liked in a man, but boy did he crash and burn.

As the only daughter of Sheikh Tariq Al-Shifa, a minor oil dealer in the Middle East, minor enough to have an annual income in the region of £75 Million, throwing money around didn't impress her. However, it wasn't asking too much that a guy should be able to pay his own tube fair on a first encounter. Regardless of where it was going.

Half Egyptian, half Kuwaiti, Amane had a very solid Islamic background, but with the commercialism that tourism and other western interests brought into the Middle East, her upbringing was quite liberal in comparison to what it may have been in a stricter more fundamental and traditional Islamic family.

Both of her parents were graduates. They met in King Fahd university in Saudi Arabia during the late sixties, married and lived in the Shiekhs homeland, Kuwait. This remained a monogamous marriage. Amane and her two elder brothers enjoyed a rich luxuriant life, mixing with the multinationals that the buoyant Kuwaiti economy attracted, until Saddam Hussien came to wreak havoc in the gulf crisis of 1991.

Amane was close to Fifteen at the time, her brothers Omar and Tariq Junior, eighteen and twenty one respectively. Naturally concerned for the family's welfare while Saddam literally set about sending the family and the whole country's assets up in smoke. The Sheikh sent his children to complete their education in England. Tariq junior, already a graduate attended business schools in Central London before departing back to Kuwait and assisting his father to rebuild and administer the family's business portfolio in 1993. Omar pursued his prospects in Medicine attending U.C.L. for the long haul of a career in surgery. Meanwhile the adolescent Amane, attended a public school in Hampstead. Her fathers wealth and connections enabling him to circumvent the red tape and waiting lists.

Being well travelled and fluent in numerous European languages, she encountered few problems finding her feet in London. The biggest setbacks in her view ,were the weather, comparable to that experienced in California or Monte Carlo as a get away, let alone the scorching temperatures reached in either of her parents homelands, secondly at the time that ' Beverly Hills 90210 ' was not readily available on terrestrial T.V.

Despite her parents wealth, Amane and her siblings refrained from lavish displays of ostentatious living and kept a very low profile whilst schooling. After the humbling experience of '91, it took a little while to resurrect the Al-Shifas fortune. Though they never lacked for anything, all three were very appreciative children as the parents verified on their occasional visits to Europe.

Now four months short of twenty one, Amane had acquired much of London's street savvy too but now possessed one of those mixed up accents that students who are well travelled or attend multinational schools always seem to have, with an American twang on everything.

She knew her way around London but choose Middlesex university to escape the rich kid mentality that seemed to infest the higher institutions in the city. Porches, sex orgies, drugs . . . she chose to stay away from such influences without having to justify her point of view which was so typical of the independent, and confident personality that she had. Part borne of her fighting for the parallel privilages her brothers had enjoyed at her age, as well as her school mates back in Kuwait while attending international school. Equally influential was growing up in her late teens till now, managing her own and some of her parents interests alone in London.

Her father had invested in property all over the capital and though he had secured the services of a competent estate management company, he trusted his daughter only. Amane had a shrewd head for business and was in the Middlesex Business School honing that talent through a joint degree in Marketing and Business Administration. Another straight A student.

Amane reached the front door of her block and turned the key in the lock. Once inside she surveyed the foyer for any post. Take away pizza leaflets and minicab cards were strewn on the foot mat, she picked them up and climbed the two flights of stairs to the door of her three bedroom flat. As she unlocked the door she observed her hanging spider plant outside her door. The mid spring sun had dried out the soil.

"I better see to that" She thought opening the door. She could hear a familiar voice speaking on the phone . . .

"Mum, please let's not go there again, I don't mean to offend you or Prashant's family but as I have said before, I'm not going through with any arranged marriage."

Amane smirked as she acknowledged Priti Parmar, one of her flat mates on the phone going over familiar ground with her one of her parents as she dumped the papers in the bin and picked up the water spray from the kitchen.

". . . . I'm only twenty two mum stop pushing me, I've not even graduated yet. I've want to get a life . . ." The phone conversation continued as Amane re-emerged from the front door having watered the plant. Priti feigned a yawn and rolled her eyes quickly to the ceiling as her friend began smiling having put down her bag and inspected her interior plants for dry soil. Amane loved plants and took good care to look after the ever greens in her house. She liked floral plants but made the concession not to have any in the house because Funmi, her second flat mate had acute hayfever.

"Say hi to your folks for me." She mimed to her friend as Priti listened impatiently on the phone.

"Amane says hi Mum." Priti relayed the greeting. "Mum says hi too and thanks again for your hospitality."

"It's a pleasure Mrs Parmar, 'Polly' is fun to have around." Amane shouted loud enough to be heard at the other end of the line.

"It's a nickname mum," Priti explained. The name was a reference to her bubbly and talkative nature. "Look I have to go O.K. I love you. Spread it to Dad and Niresh too. Bye."

Mr Parmar didn't relate to his daughters head strong character . Consequentially he found himself subconsciously spoiling his 15 year old, wiz kid-can't do no wrong - goody-goody son Niresh.

Priti was relieved to end the conversation. Unlike her two flat mates, Priti had lived in England all her life. Her family home was relatively close, in Stanmore, a suburban area of Middlesex, where generally well to do Asian professionals resided. Her parents had been living in England for some twenty five years having come over from Kenya in the early seventies. Indian by origin Priti was a nominal Hindu. but like her friend and landlady, knew her culture well, was proud of her heritage but was Hindu more out of tradition than personal conviction. Like so many other young Southern Asians, she could modulate between her culture of origin and her adopted English mode fluently and with equal effect.

Priti had chosen to study Economics in Uni and was a lazy B student, having taken a year out of academics to grasp the employment world, she came back armed with knowledge and practical experience of what she wanted to do. This kept her Dental Hygienist mother and Accountant father pleased, though the decision was all about her.

"As you already guessed Empress, that was mum flagging out that tired topic of when am I going to meet Prashant's family to make wedding plans." Priti returned the use of nicknames. Empress was given to Amane for dual reasons, first the obvious similarities the pronouncing of her name had with the designer label 'Emporio Armani and secondly they used to tease her as a rich little princess now graduated to Empress since her father had bought the flat in her name.

The flat was referred to as Amane's own empire. It was tastefully furnished without being garish. The sitting room and Amanes room were more classical though very personal. Rich deep blue carpet bedroom and Azure wallpaper to match a double bed, with a Matisse painting on the wall above the headboard a large pine double wardrobe and two matching chest of drawers with a bedside table. In the corner was a study table, on which a Sony Midi system, a Toshiba Laptop and a fax machine sat. She listened to counsel on the living room from her friends conceding that they had to live there too. The sitting room floor had wood veneer laid down and stylish rugs and skins for warmth. Two double seaters, three massive bean bags a moderate dining table and a 30 inch T.V. were the biggest features in the spacious room. The girls all agreed they wanted their own space as close as they were. They had all met two years before whilst sharing a house in Mill Hill with three other students. They gravitated towards each other more than the others and in the second semester decided to rent a place jointly just the three of them.

Their friendship grew and after eighteen months of tolerating dodgy landlords, leaking boilers and tacky decor. Amane persuaded her father to invest in some property near her college . They viewed the property at the start of December and sealed the sale in time for the January sales. Amane used £15,000 to decorate. So Habitat was the beneficiary of most of the purchasing power, while she took her two friends on a spree. It took a few weeks to redecorate but the girls moved in by early February. Funmi and Priti had a slight conscience problem with Amane's generosity which she had anticipated and dealt with accordingly.

"Listen up girls. Being the girls that you are, I can feel your apprehensions about this set up, but look we've lived together and been friends long enough to keep it real. I don't wanna live in a dodgy bedsit as much as you don't. And it just so happens that I have the means to buy a flat and do it up. I can choose who I want to live with but if it's gonna cramp your style you don't have to. I wont ask you to put up with my bullshit , as I wouldn't take any of yours. All I can say is that I will give 100% to making our friendship work and I ask that you do the same as you have been doing along.

Also Priti you gotta keep your Garage music down and Funmi you don't run your mouth about Nigeria reaching the world cup and being Olympic champions. . ." she added with mock seriousness. "Do we have a deal?"

The girls had no problem with that though Priti did need reminding from both her friends that Garage music had to be kept down and Funmi inevitably mouthing off about her brother Tayos exploits in soccer and what Nigeria were going to do to the rest of the world in the world cup she was sure they would qualify for.

They split the utility bills and things worked out well. Female bonding was evident, they would cry on each others shoulder and seek each others advice on almost every personal topic. Their diverse cultures gelled between them they had vast knowledge of the ways of the world. They could laugh at each others and their own respective customs. Three young women, knowing themselves well. Culture, customs traditions, religions. Neither making impositions on the other. Secure in who they were and where they were from, yet always wanting to grow and diversify. Modulating to one another's personalities uncontrived.

"So mums not letting up about our man, what will it take?" Amane could empathise with the arranged marriage scenario from her own background, though her parents had now accepted that she wasn't having any such meddling with her affairs. They had faith in the way they had raised their daughter and as a testimony to their beliefs, despite ample opportunity she was still a virgin. Priti on the other hand had sampled the forbidden fruit and while she only had three sexual partners, one of which was the young man that her parents were desperately trying to get her wed to, she always gave a very self assured opinion of herself.

A petite and shapely size eight, she loved to express herself and loved verbal sparring with anyone who was up to a challenge. Her name was appropriate if it sounded corny she wore her hair short looking like an Indian Halle Berry.

"I reckon Mum fears I'm so far gone that I'll stay a spinster for life, keep a cat and feed it Whiskers served with parsley for the rest of my life." They both laughed at the remote prospects of that happening. "Or even worse, that I'm a lesbian!" Priti continued.

"Priti Please!" Amane objected. With all their knowledge and awareness of the permissive world, neither of the three girls political correctness accommodated homosexuality." So marrying a Muslim would be an acceptable compromise I guess."

"What can I say Empress? I seem attracted to taboo. White guys, Black guys and Muslims. What's Omar up to this weekend?"

"Don't you stop girl? Anyway speaking of Black guys, I had an encounter with this guy on the train." Amane headed towards the kitchen to pour herself a glass of pineapple juice.

"I'm all ears. When is he coming round?"

Taking a seat on the two seater opposite Priti, Amane ignored her friends over-zealousness and continued to recite the events of the encounter with Deoye. Every detail from her discreet observation of his efforts to help the young mother on the platform, to the untimely intervention of the ticket inspector.

"Serves him right. Arrogant slob! He's probably some pervert who preys on those young Becky's that hang around Edgware station. You should've slapped his Black face and the nice profile."

"You don't give a guy credit do you Polly? There was something latently alluring about this guy. " Amane protested.

"Empress go wash your ears out! First cos you used his dirty wax ridden earphones and secondly . . ."

"Come on Polly!" Objected Amane throwing a cushion at her friend.

Priti caught the cushion ". . .And secondly cos some of that bullshit he was spinning you seemed to have stuck in your ears!" They both cracked up raining cushions at each other stopping only when a badly aimed cushion hit Amanes drink.

"Seriously Priti something about this guy set me off."

"You're a real romantic you know. I'm surprised you still hold out " Priti commented as she went to clean up the floor. "But I guess you gotta give him credit for his rap, yeah now if Prash' had some of that . . . but he's just always been the boy from around the way, just a childhood sweetheart and that's it."

"And what's wrong with childhood sweethearts?" Funmi Somefun entered the flat having heard the tailend of the conversation between her flatmates.

" Hey Funny!" Both girls greeted their friend using the nickname they had given her.

Priti's getting heat from her mom . . .

"About Prashant right?" Priti nodded having cleaned up the last of the spilt drink . Funmi sighed as she put down her shopping bags." Mums will be Mums but she should let you do your own thing as if life isn't complicated enough without their grief."

"You sound bitter about something Funny talk to the Empress." Amane said with a exaggerated patronising voice. Funmi sat next to her friend.

"Just another bad shopping day. I was looking for some shoes to wear on Saturday to that dinner party in Maida Vale I told you about."

"Uh huh, what did you get?" Priti was eager.

She had nominated herself as everyone's personal stylist. Making sure they flirted on the border line of sexy yet dignified.

"Well Russell and Bromley didn't have what I ordered, so I spent an hour and a half looking around for something else. I picked up those from 'Bally's' "

"These are wicked. I can see these working with the beige skirt suit you have." Priti had already opened both bag and box and was inspecting the elegant footwear.

"You read my mind " Funmi endorsed the combination.

"Come on that's not what's bugging you talk to me girl." Amane probed.

"You're right Empress, the guy who is hosting this thing. His Dad is a current minister back home"

"I've seen you around royalty without being ruffled. What's different about this one guy?"

"Yeah Amane. It's just that this guy's been on my case for ages. He keeps calling me on my mobile saying he has a proposition for me"

"I'll bet" Priti sarcastically interrupted.

"It's spooky, he's doing my head in. I bet he doesn't come correct and comes up with some half baked business plan which he wants me to come in on as a front for his drug money laundering and 419 deals (419 was Nigerias own brand of major big time fraud on gullible business men in England). I can do without associating myself with his kind but it presents a good chance to mingle and network with some influential people and meet up with some old friends."

"You go girl. You'll be fine" Amane reassured her.

"Thanks. I wish guys would show less predictability in trying to win the interest of a woman. He plays straight out of the rich dick heads hand book." Funmi complained contemplating the prospects of having her evening spoilt by being shadowed all night by Wole Ganiyu.

"Well, speaking of creative approaches, Amane had a close encounter of the rare kind this afternoon" Priti said in a tell tale girly voice.

"Well tell me about it" Funmi asked slapping Amane's thigh. Amane repeated her account of the events on the train.

"Hmm full marks for spontaneity but let's face it the guy is signing on. That out weighs any good points."

"Come on, give a guy a chance Funny. You don't know his circumstances " Amane protested.

"O.K. I'll break it down. How dark was he?"

"Dark"

"Bournville dark brown or milk chocky?"

"Bournville dark and a nice profile."

"Um hmm. About how old?"

"I'd say twenty one, no twenty three. He had to be twenty three tops."

"What was he wearing. Any blatant designer labels Mosh, Versace?. . ."

"No obvious labels no. Apart from a Nike cap and sneakers."

"Hi-tops or trainers?"

"Hi-tops Black."

"Was he tucked in or hanging out . . . his shirt that is!"

Amane smiled. "He was well hung I'm sure and yes, his shirt was out."

"You took in a lot of detail." Priti commented

"Well my inference is he's a West African and probably Nigerian, buys his stuff from a catalogue, on which he's running up a massive bill at some fake address, is working with an agency with a false name and maybe signing on to supplement his student grant which he claimed without going to college."

"Funmi, don't you think that's a little unpatriotic if not cynical?"

"I know Nigerian guys, trust me!"

"You two aren't selling this idea of men to me having both been there and done it already. If I listen to you all the time I'll never get me some. I ougtta throw you both out and get some red blooded hussies in here!" Amane joked as she stood up.

"If you're going to the kitchen, take this bag of shopping please Empress." Funmi managed to say through her laughter.

"I was actually going to wash my ears out but bring it anyway." Priti and Funmi carried on their bout of teasing while Amane unpacked the food shopping from the Tescos bag.

"Who's hungry?" Amane called. Both girls answered.

"Me!" breaking off their laughter.

"So Funmi, tell me bout this childhood sweetheart of yours " Priti was curious.

"Ah Priti some other time, some other time" A cushion flew over and hit her head.

"Oww!"

" Spoil sport!"

It had been a long time since he'd worn a suit but Deoye thought he carried it well . The Taupe three button single breasted wool mix suit looked smart. His other suit a navy double breasted affair was more appropriate he thought but needed a dry clean for sure. Besides, he was aware that the trousers had become shiny from wear and now looked like a different fabric from the jacket. A pure cotton light brown Van Heusen cut away collar shirt with an abstract pattered silk tie from Liberty's a Christmas present from Funmi completed the outfit.

He considered wearing the matching braces as he shuffled on the brown square toed leather loafers over his beige Burlington socks. "Nah this is only 'TEN' not Armani on New Bond Street." Deoye had enquired about vacancies after flirting with the pretty young sales assistant at TEN on the Wednesday after signing on he was advised to bring in his CV ASAP. He had tried a few shops in Brent Cross Shopping centre that day asking about vacancies. John Lewis, Fenwicks mens wear concessions and even a half hearted attempt at work in Cecil Gees, though he didn't really want to work there. He brought back his edited C.V the same day in the evening and handed it to the Menswear Floor Manager, who immediately looked over it and asked when Deoye was available for an interview.

"Right away "

"Cor you're keen, we like that! I'll tell you what can you come in midday on Friday?"

"That's fine with me." Deoye shook the mans hand observing formal etiquette. No Nigerian click this time and maintained eye contact with the guy a tall Eastender with a George Michael french crop and premature age lines precipitated by an ever present pseudo smile.

TEN was the countrys' premier fashion chain for men and women. It had been in business some fifteen years and though it had a tough time on the stock market in '91. The company survived and had flourished since. Staff were trained and assessed continuously on the features and benefits of their merchandise. A job with TEN was considered a good thing on the C.V. Deoye didn't want to screw up it was a means to an end, another hustle.

The stores had now consolidated their Spring/Summer ranges on the shop floors. But the weather wasn't assisting the sales of the neon colours and swim suits that adorned the fixtures. TEN was feeling the pinch and the Brent Cross branch had been performing under target for the last six weeks. They needed sales people, not just sales assistants, sales people to move their high price items.

Deoye arrived ten minutes early for his interview with Richard Dale the store Manager. The sales assistant that had advised him to bring in his C.V. noticed him as he strutted in and went over to inspect the formal wear.

"Looking sharp" she commented. Deoye span to reciprocate the greeting .

"Hi, thanks! You're bringing the best out of that outfit too." He instinctively evoked his charm.

"Oooh thanks. You'll be alright with that smooth talk. Who's your interview with?"

"Er the manager Richard er . . ."

"Dale!" The young assistant completed.

"Yeah that's the one. Is he gonna grill me?"

"Nah you'll be fine" The assistant assured him while arranging some formal trousers in size order. "I'll let him know you're here. What's your name ?" Deoye wanted to give her his whole name,

Adeoye Olukayode Ifedayo Olaiya with the whole Yoruba flavour representing in the house, but not wanting to suffer hearing yet another poor attempt at his name, he kept his African pride in check. He decided to super abbreviate his first name.

"Er, Oye."

The assistant returned a few minutes later with a medium built dark haired chap who looked at least 30 but was only in his mid twentys. Wearing a blue three piece suit with one of those loud fashion ties that resembled the wrappers in a box of Quality Street. Deoye couldn't figure out what was louder the tie, or the bogus smile he was wearing as he extended his hand.

"Owyer!" Pleased to meet you. Come right through. Deoye shook the extended hand firmly as he mentally winced.

"How simple can I make it? Two syllables. just two damn syllables and he screws it up!"

At first the interview itself went smoothly without any major peaks nor depressions. Not many questions were asked of him and when they were he answered confidently and correctly if not sincerely.

Richard Dale spoke about company policies and regulations, benefits and privilages most of which went straight over Deoyes head without assimilation. Deoye nodded at intervals and reciprocated the pseudo smile that his prospective boss had been constantly flashing. He was sure the manager was either cross eyed or he kept looking at the left side of his head.

"I thought I fixed my fade alright what would he know about a bad fade anyway "he dismissed.

"If you were to be successful in your application for employment with TEN, there would be two positions available. Which would you be interested in part time or full time?"

Hesitating momentarily as he could use the money that came with a full time job but could do without having his head filled with extensive facts on the washing properties of polyester cotton under garments, or other trivial information from the fashion industry. He just needed to hustle a job to fuel his dream and keep it alive.

"The part time position would suit me fine in the long term because of my academic aspirations."

"That's fine Owyer" you are on the phone aren't you? " Yes" he confirmed glancing at the C.V., "Any questions?"

"Er yeah. When can I start?" Dale laughed, a dry one."Seriously though how soon will I know?"

"We'll let you know possibly by this evening." Dales mis-pronouncing of his name was igging Deoye. he tried to sound as apologetically as possible pointing it out,

"Oh one more thing the pronouncing of the name, it's O-ye. . .Oh-ye. Kind of like a town crier" He offered the analogy. Dale rumbled the dry laugh again.

"That's a strange. Name where's it from?"

"It's Yoruba. He noticed that Dale wasn't familiar with the name of his native tribe. "Nigerian!"

"Oh right. O.K. Expect a call this evening then."

Deoye departed from the interview with an aggregate positive feeling. It seemed he had impressed without really trying.

"Hmmm, the power of physical presentation" he thought, but he still was wondering what was taking the Managers attention on the left side of his face.

He walked out of the store and sneaked a look at a full length mirror on the way. There in his ear the reason was looking at him in the face. The spade earring.

"Shit . . Shit, shit, shit I've blown it!" Taking hold of his left ear lobe with his left hand he reached up with his right hand and yanked the stud out. He let his ear lobe go he waved his hand in resignation that he'd let the job slip by.

"Tschh." Deoye kissed his teeth and waved his hand in the air. "Fuck it, they've seen me for what I am not afraid to show that I am brown and down, that's how I want it. If they don't like it they can stick the damn job!"

He loosened his tie, put his hands in his pockets and walked from the mall to Hendon Central station. Thinking all the way about getting a job and how he had screwed the interview up. Wearing an earring to an interview was slack at any rate. A shiny black onyx spade on the ear and the right hand must have been interpreted as some derivative of the Black Panther movement or some other fight the power slogan. He wouldn't make the same mistake again he'd remember to take it out for the next interview he attended. He put TEN behind him convinced he had ballsed up all prospects of employment there.

The front door slammed. "Deoye what have you been up to?"

"Uggh! Vicky. I must have dozed off." He had been circling job opportunities advertised in the previous days Evening Standard whilst in the siting room." What time is it?"

"Five O'clock. Where have you been in a suit. Did you have an interview?"

"Yeah, I went down to Brent Cross, I had an interview at TEN"

"Really how did it go?" Victoria asked putting her pile of weekend marking on the sofa next to her housemate.

"They said they would call me possibly this evening." He couldn't help sounding unenthusiastic. Victoria made for the kitchen to put the kettle on.

"If it doesn't come through, Adam's brother's just got a job in Burger King. You could try there. Do you want a cup of Coffee?"

"Thanks but no thanks Victoria . . . twice" He couldn' t understand her or Johns rate of coffee consumption and didn't appreciate being categorised with her boyfriends YTS, kid brother flipping burgers.

"I'm looking for professional work. Formal outfitting is a justifiable deviation. Burger King . . Uh uh."

"O.K. don't get stroppy I was just trying to help!"

Deoye closed his eyes to resist his inclination to give Victoria the rebuke he felt she deserved. He didn't feel able to modulate to Victorias frequency right now. He wanted to be alone with his thoughts and some cool mid-tempos. He sighed

"Are you going out tonight Victoria?"

"Well Adam's coming over later with a couple of friends we were gonna rent a movie, order a pizza and play some pictionary. Do you wanna stay around?"

'Damn' Deoye thought, As he walked down the corridor towards the stairs. He had £3 left from the £10 he had withdrawn on Wednesday. He had no intention of contributing any of it to some vegetarian pizza or watching Trainspotting or Four Weddings and a Funeral for the umpteenth time if not another Euan Macgregor or Hugh Grant film. Both of which were seen as "deliciously sexy" by Victoria.

Deoye gave credit where it was due. He accepted that George Clooney or even George Michael were good looking, but Hugh Grant had nothing going for him as far as he could see.

"Nah I'm going out tonight to see friends."

"What' you doing anything interesting?" As if they had congenial concepts of the what was considered interesting.

"We'll just be chilling somewhere!"

"Yeah it is a bit cold isn't it?" Deoye looked over his shoulder to give Victoria a scowl for her attempt at humour.

"Just joking!" Victoria apologised. Deoye climbed the stairs to take off his suit and think about what he was going to do that evening. He had just peeled to his boxers and was putting on his jeans when he heard the phone ring.

"Deoye it's for you." Good he thought maybe someone calling to tell what's going down that night. He came down stairs. Victoria was still holding the receiver. "It's TEN." She whispered with a smile as she handed the phone to him.

"Hello Deoye speaking."

"Owyer, we'd like to offer you the position of Part-Time Sales Consultant with TEN. Are you still interested?" Deoye's eyes lit up. He ignored the inevitable mispronunciation of his name. He was as surprised as he was pleased. Boy had he screwed up the interview. Dale had obviously been focusing on his ear and maybe had formed his reservations but deoye had come through. Maybe they were as desperate as he was and were going to hire the first half descent looking candidate that came along. And his presentation, spades notwithstanding, he had been more than half decent. He smiled.

"Yes I'm interested! I accept, thank you. When do I start?"

"Well officially we'd like you start on Monday but can you come in tomorrow morning for a quick induction with the Mens Floor Manager, Tony Garnett say around 8.00 a.m. and we'll take your bank details and N.I. number and all your personal details. You'll need to come in round the back entrance near John Lewis. Do you know where it is?"

"Yeah I'll find it no problem"

"Great. Come in 8 o'clock then, smart-formal but no earrings."

"Yeah! Sorry, I realised after the interview that I hadn't taken it out. Thank you for overlooking it."

"No problem tomorrow then?"

"Yeah tomorrow's fine."

"Well done you' got the job!" Victoria had lingered while he received the news.

"Uh-huh." Deoye confirmed reservedly. For sure Dale had seen the earring whether he knew what it represented remained to be seen. He felt burdened that he had added to the colour of his skin as a handicap Black people are always carrying, by the abberation with his stud, before he had even started the job.

"Great! New Nigga with an attitude" his extreme paranoia called out in his mind.

"You don't sound too chuffed"

"Don't get me wrong. I'm thankful for the job but it's just temporary a means to an end. I'm just hustling it."

"You mean you're going to chuck it in soon?"

"The media's where I wanna be Vicky. Like I said I'm just hustling this." Repeating himself, Deoye contemplated his new job; Standing four hours at a stretch, in a tie and some hard soled shoes, for sub £5.00 per hour.

"Who's hustling who"? he thought to himself. Still he could hold his head high and avoid the depressing fortnightly trips to the dole office. It was a new beginning at a weekend he felt the urge to share his positivity.

Dialling a number from memory he watched Vicky in the kitchen make her coffee with wishy-washy non-fat milk. Yuk! he thought.

An answering machine message began playing in his ear.

"Hi this is Femi, Sorry I can't answer the phone right now . . . "Hello!" Femi answered the phone.

"Femo why you dey use answering machine to deceive person like say you no dey house ?" Deoye evoked the pigeon English.

"Man me, nah some fast action dey go down." Femi groggily replied.

"You're a dog bro!" Deoye switched to an East coast American accent knowing that Femi was with a girl.

"Players gotta do his thang. You know what I'm sayin'?" Femi kept the flow.

As a postman, Femi's occupational hazard was becoming familiar with too many people or more specifically too many girls for his own good. He lived on the outskirts of and delivered post to Graham Park Estate. A large housing area in North West London.

Femi knew where every girl with passable looks lived on the estate. Nigerian, Asian, West Indian, Zambian, Oyingbo . . . whatever and if he hadn't made a move to hit on them already, he had their number. Working in the early hours of the day up until 2.00pm left plenty of time for him to indulge in his favourite pastime . . . lying down, usually with a girl from the estate or from the nearby Hendon College or Middlesex University dorms who had been suckered into giving it up.

He targeted impressionable girls. He had what they liked to see, mobile phone, designer labels on clothes not necessarily designer clothes, gaudy gold chain, rented his own one bedroom flat and his prize H reg Golf GTI convertible . . . with alloy wheels and a booming sound system.The complete tools for his sex driven lifestyle.

"In and out, no strings just my tingz " That was his catch phrase. The two met in a sorting office Xmas '95 both temps at the time and working through the night shared their experiences of Nigeria and thus bonded. Though they had very contrasting opinions on many topics, they seemed to have an understanding when expressing their sense of humour. Femi knew how to party . If there was something going on that night 'Femo' was the man and Deoye felt like mingling.

"What's going on tonight?"

"Well me and this piece of arse, that I just put to sleep, are gonna kick another few rounds when she comes to, before I send her home limping. I'll trip down to Iceni's by say midnight and collar some other babe to see me through till the morning."

Deoye considered the £3.00 odd in his pocket. Even if he wanted to he wasn't getting into any club tonight. He still had his 'giro' to cash which had arrived at the second post though not delivered by Femi, but too late. He wasn't going to make it to any post office.

"O.K. you can count me out."

"Wassup your broke ass can't afford it? I'll cover you?"

"Who's broke? I got a job!"Deoye bluffed. Femi always criticised him for being morose and bad company since he hadn't had a job. And though Femo would cover his friend on occasion, Deoye felt guilt, as if he was sponging off his friend.

"Oh yeah? Since when?"

"Tschh! I've been working at TEN at Brent Cross for like two weeks."

"Yeah right, how come I've never seen you in there?"

"Cuz you're probably too busy looking at the girls working there" Deoye reinforced his bluff.

"Word! Hey what's that light skin girls name, fine with a weave, bout 5'3" packed chest? Femi whispered.

"I don't know!"

"What do you mean you don't know?"

"I don't know? I don't piss the same place I eat! Besides it's quality not quantity for me." Deoye tried to turn defence into attack with a dig at his friends rampant promiscuity.

"You' just slack that's all and speaking of quality , I asked you to hook me up with your cousin Funmi" Femi wasn't phased.

"She ain't my cousin, how many times must I tell you. Besides you ain't got it" Femi was treading on a soft spot.

"Then how come you ain't gettin' some there then ? If I were in your shoes I'd be there and be singing like Joe . . " Don't Wanna Be A Player No More, I think I found someone . . ."

"Femo go back to sleep!" Femi had hit a raw nerve and he knew it. As a wicked exponent of sarcasm he liked to wind up his friend. The girl next to him stirred.

"Uh-oh. Time for the booticall you know what I'm saying?" He whispered."Round three is about to begin, gotta go my dick's gettin hard."

"Later man." Deoye heard Femi schmoosing "come here baby " before he hung up.

In preparation for a night in listening to his vast C.D. collection, he reached inside his jacket hanging in the landing for his earphones. while extracting them from the inside pocket a piece of paper dropped, it landed reverse side up. His own hand writing showed a familiar telephone number.

"Have you finished on the phone." Victoria called out from the kitchen having set a "Lean Cuisine" meal in the microwave.

"Nah just one more quick call." Deoye held the phone receiver between shoulder and chin as he dialled Funmi's number. He slid down to the floor as the phone rang and pulled his knees up to his chest. He could feel his heart pounding against his thigh and cursed his lack of composure. Nearly four months since he saw or spoke to Funmi he didn't know what response he would get.

"Hello!" Something about the voice that answered sounded familiar, it wasn't Funmi.

"Hi, can I speak to Funmi please?"

Amane's memory banks were evoked. She knew it was a Black guy on the phone by the distinct tone, she tried to think who it was.

"Who shall I say is speaking?" Deoye was sure he'd heard the voice before. The unplaceable accent , the slight American twang . . .

"Deoye, please tell her it's Deoye."

"O.K. Hold on." Amane by now was racking her brain. The name wasn't familiar but could the phone distort someone voice that much? She just couldn't put a face to the voice." Funmi!" she shouted. "You got a call."

"Who is it?" Funmi shouted back.

"A guy called Deoye." Amane had no problem pronouncing most names, as a result of her exposure to the varied cultures of the world. As Funmi came to take her call Amane whispered. "Do we know him?"

"I don't think so, he's my cousin." Funmi replied as she took the cordless receiver from her friend with a dimpled smile. "D !long time no see where have you been?" Deoye heard Funmis reply to her friend and was responding in his mind

" I'm not your cousin, I'm not your cousin".

"I've er been around the world and aye aye aye couldn't find my baby . . . so I'm callin you instead"

"Sweet mout! You'll never change." Funmi was still smiling as Priti and Amane were now eaves dropping on her conversation. She tried to dismiss their enthusiasm."What have you been up to?"

"Well since I lost my job at Simpson and Blake that Ad agency, I've been hustling here and there. Just tryin' to get something going. So I got myself a part time number with TEN at Brent Cross . It's not great but it goes on the C.V. even though it is a deviation."

Funmi retraced in her mind where Deoye was at since they last spoke. He had been temping with an advertising agency for a few months up until Xmas and seemed to be stable. But always complained about the hyper sales atmosphere and lack of real people at the firm despite the £9.50 per hour he received.

He didn't enjoy it and had a run in with his supervisor. Who informed his agency that his negativity was detrimental to office morale, and his lack of motivation had affected his output. The truth was the boss fancied himself as Chris Evans and every one had to stoop to kiss his ass or be ejected. Though his work was exceptional, Deoye didn't laugh at his tasteless jokes, challenged his overt sexism, didn't share intimate details of his own private sexual exploits, couldn't stand the way seemingly every other employee punctuated each sentence with a swear word, or went to the pub on every Friday night to drink themselves paralytic, have a curry and throw it all up . . . with the lads.

Under those conditions he didn't want to be a team player. Things came to a head when Deoye wouldn't put up £15.00 for the offices Xmas bash. And told his boss up front that a night in a seedy Soho joint with his colleagues didn't constitute in his opinion a night of entertainment. His boss gave him a bum rap and terminated his employment just before Xmas. Hence the employment agency hadn't found him any work since.

Though Funmi believed Deoye, she did feel he could learn the art of diplomacy in the work place as it was clearly an attribute that he lacked and would need to acquire.

"So welcome to the retail world, like you say it's a deviation but something doing."

"We'll I'm not exactly in the same league as you come on, TEN and DKNY?" Deoye made reference to Funmi's job.

"I only go in one day a week now. The customers are sweet and you know they tip well."

"I bet they do. Met any stars recently?"

"A few but we play it down."

"Which comes easily when your brother is a star I guess. Tayo's making waves in Europe. He was all over the papers last month when he scored two goals against Villa. Has he been in touch?"

"Yeah he's doing well. I'm really pleased for him." Funmi didn't want to reveal the extent of her true joy for her brothers success as she knew that Deoye could have equally been a footballer if his father had been more reasonable." He calls often. Says he doesn't have your number though, let me take it now before I forget. Deoye gave his number and they talked laughed and reminisced about current affairs anecdotes and the child hood they shared. There was an imbalance in emotional investment. Deoye the idealist romantic gauged girls against Funmi. She was the barometer as far as he was concerned he wondered still what might had been between them if he had a little more fortune and they weren't practically family.

Funmi the realist recognised that Deoye was an OK guy, though a little rugged. He had substance too, but her life had always been precise and definite even without the fact that she was 10 months older, his shit wasn't together. He was too scattered, too insecure.

"So when are we gonna hook up?" Deoye was convinced he had redeemed himself from his sabbatical from his long time female friend. Funmi was wise to him

"Tell you what, let's pencil in a date just before Xmas." She teased. "Make it a good round year."

"I'm sorry. I just needed to get my shit together." Always the score Funmi thought. "So what are you doing tonight? We can jam somewhere."

"We always jam somewhere and do something you wanna do. I'm calling this one." Funmi remembered her soirée at Maida Vale hosted by Wole Ganiyu. Deoye could front as her partner for the evening.

"What are you doing tomorrow night around 8.30 down?" Priti gave Funmi a thumbs up sign as she read her friends mind.

"Nuthin." Deoye declared

"O.K. Be here for 8.00 p.m. I got a little private affair in Maida Vale we can attend together. I know you don't like those Naija gatherings but you owe me Deoye. We can always fade away on our own if it gets too dry." He made a point of never meeting Funmi around her friends. He felt that they deprived him of the one to one close camaraderie almost laddish banter that they shared, but he had to make a compromise to rekindle his friendship.

"I'll be there 8.00 p.m. Sharp. Are your sweet sounding flatmates gonna be in?" Funmi threw the question to her flatmates.

"Yeah we'll be here!" Priti and Amane shouted in unison, no further light shed on who had answered the phone, which had been bugging Deoyes mind since he made the phone call.

"I'm curious you know what they say 'bout birds of a feather hmmm."

"You're incurable Deoye." Funmi glanced at her friends as the image of Deoye with one of her friends flashed in her mind . "Dress smart but not formal. I know you' got the stuff."

"Gimme your address then." Funmi obliged.

"Right! It's a date Funmi see you tomorrow, luv ya."

"Love you too, bye."

Deoye hung up the phone. Good. Tonight I can chill I'll get my groove on tomorrow. He thought.

"Vicky the phones free" He called out as he bound up the stairs while thinking of what he was going to wear tomorrow night. The induction with TEN was in the morning. He hoped it went quickly, he hoped the whole day went quickly. "Bring on Saturday night . Tonight I'll chill tomorrow another level.

"Yeah I'll bust a little BlackStreet" he concluded."No Diggity."

"Well played Funny." Priti praised her friends tact in arranging an escort for her function and held up her hand as Funmi acknowledged the hi-five." So which cousin is this then?"

"Er he's not exactly a cousin. You know how it is, you grow up with someone, family friends and all that." Her friends nodded, part in empathy, patronisingly.

"Hmm so you wanna tell me bout that childhood sweetheart you mentioned the other day?" Priti probed. She was spot on.Funmi's complexion concealed a blush, she smiled and got up.

"Oh no you don't girlfriend." Sit yourself back down right now and fill us in." Amane was just as curious and shoved her friend gently back onto the sofa.

Funmi filled in her friends on how Deoye, his sister Bolanle, her brother Tayo and herself were close in Nigeria. About the death of Deoyes mother how his father was such a contrast to her own fair thinking Pop. About how they shared dreams and how Deoye had a good heart, but couldn't get his act together. When she finished talking she still seemed to be staring into the past.

"Hmm sounds like a real nice guy you sure you're over him?" Amane noticed her friends gaze.

"There's nothing to get over Princess, really. I wish he could fix himself up." Funmi snapped out of her trance and tried to play down any suspicions her friends may have had that there was more to her relationship with Deoye.

"Well fix me up then." Priti insisted

"Get in line Polly." Amane staked her claim.

"Look at the two of you and you ain't even seen him yet." Funmi objected."If you don't behave, I' ll give you both a bad report."

"You said he's alright looking didn't you."

"Tall, dark and moderately handsome."

"Uh huh. I know your taste, that's fine with me." Amane teased. Neither of them had ever dated a guy that either of them had previously been out with, it just never happened without it being a spoken rule.

"We'll see him tomorrow night, to verify how tall, how dark and just how moderately handsome, Forgive me if I'm clock watching from seven down." Priti wasn't letting up.

"You're both mad." Funmi had missed Deoye a lot and tried not to let on to her friends with little success. She looked forward to his companionship and sensed Deoye had a soft spot for her.

Amane still hadn't figured it out. The voice was more distinct every time she played it over in her mind. She looked at her ultra flat Longines wrist watch. Twenty six hours and counting, bring on Saturday night.

Chapter Three

"Near post Some Fun! Near post!" Tayo curled the ball hard and low as instructed. "Oh Yes!" Karl Reinhoff saluted his goal as his deft touch beat the keeper to convert Tayos inch perfect pass.

English was a chosen lingua Franca at Amsterdam F.C. As Every body spoke it as a second language. Eighteen first team squad members were going through their paces in the morning practice session, which as ever was as ever very competitive. Eleven first team places were up for grabs in tomorrows crunch game with Feyenord. Nobody was applying themselves more thoroughly than Tayo, he was eager to claim a regular first team place in the domestic scene, which despite his brilliant performances in the UEFA cup he just couldn't secure.

Coach Rene Van Langen rotated his squad players though he worked with a core of seven or eight players he generally played a 3-5-2 formation but switched to 4-3-3 for the clubs European games. With the later formation he accomodated Tayo with devastating effect. Amsterdam were in the quarter finals of the UEFA cup and having beaten Aston Villa 3-1 in the away leg in Birmingham courtesy of a dazzling performance by Tayo, were as good as through to the semi-finals. But Tayo was frustrated at his lack of first team performances. He had spent nearly four years with Amsterdam and learnt his trade. No longer a naive rookie, at twenty three he was good enough to command a first team place. But Amsterdam not being a big city club, though one of Europe's top five, never had the resources to keep players. They invested in their youth policy, grooming tomorrow's stars and selling them on to keep afloat.

Tayo knew that with just over a season left on his contract, the inevitable offer of another short term paltry contract with a renumeration a third of what he could command in Italy Spain or even England, was the best they could offer him as he was not considered a first team regular. The scenario was too familiar, he was a pawn in the game ,it was a matter of time he was sure he would be put up for sale soon. However his desire to just play football may force the clubs hand.

Nigeria were as good as through to the world cup finals with Brazil the holders and France the hosts. He had to be a part of that squad, to facilitate his chances regular first team football was essential. Ikpeba, George and Babangida had head starts on him as the wide players and Amocachi was still doing his thing in Turkey. If it was all about money he could wait till his contract expired at the end of the next season and move, with possibly a bumper pay out as a free agent. However business sense ment that he had to be in the shop window playing, which would also enhance his selection chances for France 98. The club expected a fee in the region of at least £4 million. It was better for both parties, player and club that he left. But the waiting was the toughest part.

"Another nice cross Tayo" The coach called out. Tayo just acknowledged the praise and kicked a divot into the turf. "Right a quick session of penalty taking then that's it. Five each O.K. Defenders over the other end." Frankie Kieft the under twenty one international walked up to Tayo.

"It's bugging you I can tell Some Fun."

"What is?" Tayo played dumb.

"Your situation with the league and Europe you know what I mean." Tayo tried to observe club politics not wanting to fuel any rumours.

"It's not the ideal situation but I'll persevere and work on my game and hope to make a break through. Thanks for your concern though Frankie."

Tayo jogged over to the penalty area to practice his spot kicks. Patrick Schiesner the clubs regular penalty taker had just hit five straight. Using alternate feet. His team mates jeered his arrogance.

The rest of the forwards and midfielders took theirs in turn, testing their keeper who did well to keep out a good number. Tayo drilled his first two kicks left footed into the bottom right hand corner placed the next two in the left hand corner. He let his dimpled smile break loose as a devious thought came to mind.

He placed the ball on the spot, took three steps back , still smiling he put his hands on his hips.

"Come on Some Fun let's see what you got." keeper Hans Hastrop challenged. Tayo took two steps forwards, Hastrop crouched, Tayo swung back his right foot his posture suggested he was going to place the ball to his keepers left. Hastrop anticipated this and began to move. As he completed his sprawl he saw Tayo pivot his ankle and toe poke the ball into the top right corner. Hastrop cursed in Dutch.

"Q.E.D. there you go." Tayo extended his smile. As his team mates and coach applauded his maverick method of depositing the ball in the net.

"O.K. that's enough for today." Van Langen called out. Six months ago Tayo would have grabbed one of the youth team players and practiced his skills, close control, crosses in motion, free kicks or more penalties. But now he could feel his spirit was waning. He loved the game of soccer. It was always his dream to be a pro, now he had reached his first cross roads. Amsterdam had looked after him well and nurtured him. Yet at twenty three he was still seen as potentially great by the club. Though he conceded that he wasn't the finished article, his development wasn't being helped by sitting on the bench time after time.

He considered the life he had made for himself in Amsterdam was very privileged. A luxurios flat overlooking the river. His car was re-leased every year being club sponsored Lexus Coupe. The Nightclub scene he was the man. He loved dancing and music Tayo had the moves and would always run the floor. The city seemed to be too small, he was recognised every where. Accepted, it was part and parcel of being a professional footballer, however he could never go out and be alone to himself.

Autograph hunters, groupees, press men always in his face he had achieved pop star status with his trade mark dimpled smile and new goal celebration. It was bitter sweet though as he weighed up the good points with the bad. Women, babes, girls. He had them on tap but Amsterdam was notorious its vice and prostitution.

When he first arrived in the capital his naivety was exploited. A young girl of barely sixteen seduced him with little resistance as this was his first taste of Oyingbo, he gave it up with no qualms.

It turned out that later the girl turned to prostitution and threatened the club with selling the story to the press. The clubs lawyers settled the affair with a payout to the young prostitute. Three months later the same girl was found dead with her pimp. Hyperdermic needles everywhere the two had O.D'd on pure crack having spreed on drug cocktails with the out of court settlement payout for their silence. The club reprimanded Tayo for his lack of discretion and he had a curfew imposed. As a result he learnt to apply his libido with more tact and since dated a string of beautiful girls mostly white models or rich women who were often slightly older than him. His current interest was a half dutch, half Surinam, beauty named Sofia.

Sofia was a twenty one year old model. Tall with a great poise, her looks were hot. Potentially she had a lot going for her but had a reputation for a fiery attitude and single minded ruthless ambition to succeed big. She was no bimbo.

Tayo coped with her attitude at first thinking that her work between the sheets served as adequate compensation . . . Besides she did look good on the arm and stopped him from bed hopping. But after they had been together eight months, the relationship seemed to have a serious twang to it. Sofia had by now recognised Tayos commercial appeal which was an added bonus to her genuine attraction to him.

They met at an Autumn fashion show in Paris while he was on a pre-season tour. That was the longest he had been without being promiscuous. He was convinced if Sofia found out he was cheating she would scratch the girls eyes out and cut off his seeds. As good as she was for him. He still had reservations on the relationship. Sofia was what he called an Oyingbo. She didn't nurture his culture. At first she seemed too caught up in her own self marketing. She liked to be seen at the power parties and helped him spend his £4000 a week salary which even without her ostentatious taste, was getting harder and harder to stretch. Of all the people he came into contact with on a regular basis, associates, team mates, agents he had to concede she was the only real friend. Despite the pampering and attention he received when he first arrived at Amsterdam FC, he couldn't trust any of the players, he always felt hustled.

People around him had the clubs interests at heart not his, which was all thoroughly professional he was the second fiddle who was about to fulfil his purpose for the club, making a fat amount of money to invest in other stars. No one really got to his personal side which in his maturing as a footballer and more so a person had suffered.

Tayo trudged off the field down the tunnel to the dressing room. The normal banter of a mens locker room filled the air. Tayo was alone in his thoughts as he changed to shower. He watched his team mates attempt his celebration dance and laughed.

"You just don't have the moves he called out with a distorted Nigerian accent."

"Come and teach us Schiesner called back." Tayo declined the invitation and headed for the showers.

The team sheet for the game with Feyenord was posted on the notice board in the players lounge. The players congregated there and departed. Tayo approached the board as Kieft left with a smile on his face.

"Too bad Some Fun!"

"Arrogant swine!" Tayo thought as the Dutch national under twenty one sweeper/skipper confirmed his thoughts Subs bench again. I can't take any more of this I'm asking for a transfer. Tayo stormed out of the players lounge and headed for the managers office. On approaching he began to have second thoughts about his decision should he call his agent? Nah. He didn't have a Jerry Maguire relationship with his agent. He'd just be thinking of the cut he would make out of it. He needed to speak to someone with his feelings at heart.

"I'll call Funmi on this she'll give it to me straight. I hope she's got Deoyes number too."

Waking up with a sense of purpose for the first time in four months motivated Deoye. His pride delayed his application for unemployment benefit for two months but when his savings quickly eroded and he found himself leaning on his friend Femi too often he put in his claim.

He had set the alarm for 7.00 a.m. But he was awake before it sounded. He turned on his walkman radio. It was pre programmed for 96.9 F.M. The sounds of LL Cool J's 'Doin it' flowed. Deoye sung along meaning every lyric as he thought about the pleasurable dream he had over the night.

Purely erotic, he had made mutually gratifying love some faceless Black girl with the baddest figure, As he rerun the scenes in his mind it was a packed black body but the face belonged to the classy babe he had met on the train on Wednesday.

"Hmm freaky but nice" he thought."They gotta invent dream videos" He got up and sat on the edge of his bed and delayed doing his routine fifty press ups, as his morning hard on would have limited the proper execution. He waited a while for his blood to recirculate before he begun.

One . . .Two . . . Three. He heard foot steps on the stairs then the bathroom door shut.

"I hope John's just taking a piss" Ten . . . Eleven . . . Then he heard another set of heavier foot steps. Then a knock at his bedroom door.

"Yeah come in." he called out continuing his exercise. John Fuller stepped into Deoye's room and the bathroom door shut.

"Ah, far too exerting at this time of the morning for me" he commented as his house mate locked on number twenty.

"How you doing John?" Deoye gasped trying to figure out who was in the bathroom but he had a notion that John was about to disclose to him.

"Alright I suppose. I had a mad night last night one of my colleagues had a leaving do in town. Karen came along then came back with me . . ."

"And she's in the bathroom now yeah . . ?"

"Yeah just to let you know in case you were going anywhere this morning."

"I 'm going to an induction with TEN at Brent Cross actually. I gotta be there for eight O'clock this morning."

"What you got a job? Nice one! Nice one Deoye! You can sort me out with some discount then."

"Thanks John but I was sure you were a Ben Sherman man through and through" Deoye decelerated reaching forty five."

"I guess you can apply for a management position there after six months or so?"

Deoye 's muscles relaxed as he collapsed on forty six.

"Why do white folk always think we should rest on our laurels and not pursue our dreams and ambitions"?

He asked himself silently. "It's a part time job while I look to do my main thing John. I told you that and I will stay focused."

"O.K. well good luck to you." John couldn't understand Deoye's apparent defensiveness.

"Yeah thanks John. Is Karen gonna be much longer cos I gotta shower now?"

"You don't wanna be late do ya. I'll call her out." Deoye didn't mean to be short with John but he wished John would listen to his individual aspirations rather than assume every black persons motivations were just to get any job and be content with the privilege.

"These aren't the we shall overcome ages. Yet people seem to smirk consciously or subconsciously over any aspirations we have of reaching the top outside of sports. Unlike our brothers and sisters the other side of the Atlantic who can be seen making in roads in all realms of professionalism. So much for equal opportunities." Deoye thought still peeved by John's remark.

After a quick hot shower Deoye dressed smart but casually in chinos a blue Polo shirt and a pair of cleated moccasins. "Uh huh that's appropriate" he told himself looking in the mirror. "You gotta go he added" and removed his Onyx earing. He finally decided to leave his shirt out of his trousers and splashed on a little Antaeus cologne as an extension of his personal hygiene.

"7.20 still time to grab a munch before I leave."

Deoye arrived at the back door of TEN at the same time as some of his new colleagues. He felt conspicuous not being formally attired as he waited in the staffroom for Tony Garnett. He observed the many staff in their melee. Most of them, he deduced from their conversations were students on part time hours. They looked a lively bunch of people as they caught up with the weeks news suspiciously eyeing his apparent frown.

"New guy huh?" A male voice came from behind him. Deoye turned to acknowledge the Indian guy standing behind him smartly dressed with a well groomed goatee.

"Yeah. I start on Monday, I'm in to see Tony Garnett for an induction".

"Are you on menswear?"

"Yep that's right ten to two, Monday to Friday."

"Cool. The name is Sunil."

"Deoye. You can call me Oye for short."

"Deoye?"

"Right first time. I'm impressed!" Sunil smiled.

"See you later." He left the staffroom and headed towards the shop floor as Tony Garnett came in.

"Owyer good to see ya. Well done on getting the job. Do you wanna come through?"

"Hi, its er Oye." He corrected Garnett offering his hand. Garnett ignored the gesture and held the door open for Deoye to walk through. He took Deoye on to the shop floor and explained the individual departments and sections of the mens floor. A lot of the information imparted was obvious though there were a few terms new to Deoye. Garnett reeled off product information of the new Spring/Summer range with unbridled pride focusing on features and benefits of each garment or fabric. Asking his new starter to answer the questions periodically.

"So this is our new range of shoes. Though we still maintain our classics on the fixtures over there."

He picked up a pair of 70s throw back loafers. "Here we go! This is our best seller this season so far. They're the dogs bollocks, that's why I got pair. £49.99. Come in two colours brown and black . What would you say is the biggest feature having a look at the shoe?" Garnett handed the shoe to Deoye who looked at the shoe and took in the genuine leather upper logo, the stacked heel. The garish silver band across the upper instep.

"The seventies mould makes it fashion responsive . . ?"

"No you donut. It's got a leather upper!"

"I noticed the vero curo sign in the shoe but isn't that like saying a £12,000 car has a steel chassis? Besides you could get a full leather shoe for £50.00." Deoye defended his answer.

"Well it's not taken for granted that all shoes are leather and this is TEN a bench mark for style, quality and fashion."

Deoye conceded he could tell this guy was clearly sold on his job and could do without another aberration to rival the earstud affair.

"True." He tasted his tongue change colour to that of his general complexion. I see your point."

"Good!" Garnett continued the induction breaking down details of the how and why of TEN.

Deoye tried to remain attentive telling himself repeatedly, it was just a hustle.

"Right this is Sunil he runs the formal wear, which is where you will be working.

Sunil tell Oye what's the crack with the formal section then send him through to the office to complete his details."

Sunil offered his hand .They shook the three tier street shake. " I like this guy". Deoye thought.

"Do you work here full time?" Sunil gave Deoye a look that said " please!"

"No I'm at Westminister university studying Business Methods and Accountancy final year, couldn't do any more hours star."

"So this is just a hustle right?" They looked in each others eyes. Sunil's affirmation was silent.

"You said it not me." Sunil made a fist and showed the side of it. Deoye reciprocated and they touched fists.

Sunil switched to work mode and gave his new colleague a light hearted yet thorough, ten minute low down on the product information of the mens formal wear, before Deoye completed his personal details in the administration office. He was about to leave when Garnett caught up with him.

"Before you go Oh - ye, is that right?"

"Spot on Tony."

"Great, I'm about to give a team talk if you're not in a hurry, it'd be a good chance for you to experience the way we motivate the staff and make them aware of the daily focus such as sales targets and security issues."

"Sure no problem." They walked through to the shop floor and the staff automatically separated into two groups, behind the counter and in front of it. The hierarchy and the plebs. Deoye noticed all the managers behind the counter were white.

Sunil motioned with his head for Deoye to come over. Garnett proceeded to address the staff as Deoye listened while surveying his new co workers.

The hierarchy consisted of Garnett and two women. The first an atractive looking brunette who seemed shy and out of her depth. Next to her a shorter business like looking woman stood with a note book out looking over her glasses at the crowd in front of her. The crowd consisted of four Asian girls, one Mediteranian looking guy, two Mediteranian looking girls, One white guy, two Asian guys including Sunil and a Sister.

Deoye looked over at the black girl seeking some kind of acknowledgment for representing, It didn't come. Deoye took in the rest of sisters features. She was O.K. looking, wearing one of those sassy bobs that Black girls wear. She had attitude Deoye could see, another plus in his mind.

He subtly adjusted his posture to survey the girls figure. "Pow! What a bust. So that's what Femo was talking about. Girls chest wasn't so big but it stood up like it was the curve on a capital P." He covered his mouth to hide the smile that had busted out.

"You noticed Arlenes assets then." Sunil had noticed Deoyes surveilance.

"Hmm both of them." They laughed at the same time, as the crowd responded to a joke that Garnett had told. The rest of the staff joined them in their laughter. Deoye and Arlenes eyes met still no positive nod of solidarity. The laughter died down.

"Right one more thing before we open. Meet Oye over here he starts on menswear Monday can we give him a big TEN welcome." Garnett pointed in his direction .

"Hi Oye came a female dominated response."

"Hi y'all." Deoye smiled back.

"Hi y'all? This is TEN, Brent Cross, London. Not some American diner bar."

Laughter broke out again. Arlene seemed to be leading it. The joke was on Deoye.

No problem he thought this is one big hustle that's all, one big hustle.

Sheresse St.Andre applied a mild foundation on to her already flawless skin. She looked up at the clock. Her daughter, Tamar watched impatiently.

"When's Daddy coming?" Sheresse found it difficult to explain to her daughter, her fathers absenteeism. Calvin was a wanna be Yardie, too into womanising to even make the dedication to the occupation. Sheresse was just one of a few baby mothers Calvin had. Sheresse wanted a man, when she met Shokoya in 1991 he tripped her with his big spending and made the proposal for the marriage transaction.

Eighteen at the time and already living alone, £2500 sounded a good price for the deal. She bought herself a B reg.Q plated Escort XR3i for £2000. The rest she blew away on riders and other accessories of her Ragga Girl past. Shokoya kept in touch regularly fufilling his conjugal rites as her husband until he legalised his stay. Sokoyas dubiously acquired wealth grew and he treated his wife more frequently. Paris trips, designer shopping sprees and twenty first birthday party at the Granaries. He also covered the finance on her Peugeot 306 XSi. (She wrote off the Escort in six months having only acquired basic insurance). But Sheresse loved her independence and kept Shokoya from moving in.

She met Calvin at a party. His good looks and gold tooth helped his cause. He was looking for a meal ticket to stay in the country having come over fresh from J.A. in 93 sponsored by his big brother he was meant to stay with an older relative to set him on a straight path but he never bothered to look her up. Instead he played on the novel appeal that his authentic Jamaican culture had on the wanna be ragga girls in the community. He sowed his oats far and wide but Shokoya had already beaten Calvin to using Sheresse to legalise his stay. He had to look elsewhere to complete his plan having already got Sheresse pregnant. This didn't help his already tilted opinion of Africans.

When Sheresse disclosed that she was married. His game plan was revealed he swore he'd kick the Nigerians ras. He was out of luck and nothing more than a loser sponging off his many baby mothers' spread around South London. " Running a lickle drugs here and there to make ends meet."

Girls began to find his game tired and Sheresse didn't give him any play whenever his sorry arse showed up.

She lived the lie that Shokoya was Tamars father. He was the one who brought her clothes and presents, covered the trip to Disney land Paris and presented a good material image of a father. Calvin was content to sponge off the benefits that the deceit brought and it meant one less baby mother to provide for, not that he did provide for any of them.

"Make the foolish African stay there. Dyam fool." He'd say ."When I cetch him I'm gonna bus his ras".

"When's Daddy coming."Tamar repeated playing with her braids.

"He's going to meet us in MacDonalds this morning for breakfast. So stop disturbing me Tamar and we'll meet him there."

"I wanna Happy Meal ,Can I have a happy meal Mummy?"

"Say please Tamar."

"Please can I have a Happy Meal Mummy?"

"Tamar it's breakfast! They don't serve Happy Meals at breakfast." Tamar sat on her mothers bed in the two bedroom flat and sulked. Her mum continued to apply her make up and smiled at her three year old replica. Tamar looked so much like her mum it facilitated the lie she lived. She was very advanced. Her mother treated her as a friend more than a daughter. She began reading before she was three and her Grand mother adored and spoiled her. Sheresse stood up in her negligee and went to the wardrobe to pull out her beauty consultants work uniform.

After gaining a diploma in beauty therapy, Sheresse worked at a Fashion Fair concession in an Oxford Street store. Excellent at her trade, she was very professional and enjoyed the glamour attached to the job even if it was only three days a week, Monday, Friday and Saturday. She slipped on her two piece suit. And told herself she could be the corporate woman she wanted to be as she put on co ordinating shoes. Tamar looked at her fully dressed mother proudly and got up to get her coat.

"You're Pretty mommy."

"So are you honey, so are you."

Shokoya strolled into MacDonalds 10.48a.m.Some twenty minutes late. He went upstairs to meet his ex wife. Sheresse looked at her watch as he approached and kissed her teeth.

"You know I start work at 12.00 but you come in late Folabi". He beamed his white smile.

"Sorry eh, I had some business matters to attend to."

"Yeah right like your daughter ain't your business !" Sheresse lied with the emotional blackmail tip. Afolabi kissed Sheresse on the cheek as she pulled away. He admired her feisty ways and appreciation for material things. His Nigerian girlfriends didn't have the same spirit somehow and would milk a man dry and move on to the next. Sheresse was fine and she could throw down.

"Where's my little girl?"

"Daddy ! Daddy!" Tamar came running over with a balloon in one hand and a flag in the other. "Daddy I got MacDodalds bwekfast and a balloon".

"Ah my girl, my Daddys Girl". He smothered Tamar with kisses and looked at her little face beaming. "You just look like your mother shah!" Shokoya loved and spoiled Tamar as any father would. He was none the wiser that Sheresse was playing him through fear that he'd cut her off without any thought or compunction. He now attained his legal right of abode, she had nothing else to hold onto him with. She under estimated her attraction, Shokoya fell for Sheresse big time and though she never meant to have a child with Calvin or anyone, it worked out conveniently for her using Shokoya.

Calvin wasn't around when Tamar was born. However though he missed the birth, Shokoya on the other hand was at large during the pregnancy and showed up at the hospital with flowers fruit presents and all. She couldn't bring herself to tell him the truth, he'd step for sure knowing his contempt for "Jamos". A summer of rampant passion in '93 with Calvin meant her beloved daughter Tamar was the pawn holding all aces in the dicey game she played.

Sheresse had measured Shokoya for a jacket and it had a snug fit. Unwittingly he loved to wear it and wore it well. It was her secret she couldn't let anyone know but her sister Dionne. Her baby father was a pretty boy wanna be Yardie with nothing going for him. Her mother had admonished her against such Jamaican guys with extreme bias."Don' fall for no Yardie bwoy you nah." The words played over in her head but she reassured herself all was in control.

Sheresse watched and finished her breakfast as Shokoya played with Tamar giving her the toys he had bought for her.

"She's going to stay with my Mum today. It's her cousins fifth birthday party."

"Yeah! Are you going to a party Remi ?" He called Tamar by the Yoruba name his Mum had suggested when he told her that he was a father. "What are you wearing, has Mummy bought you a new dress?"

"She don't need one Folabi she hasn't worn half of the stuff that she's got as it is."

"I'm gonna dance when I get to Tevins party."

"Show Daddy how you're gonna dance Tamar." Tamar moved in rythmn to Brandy's Sittin up in my room singing along as she grooved.

Shokoya encouraged her.

"Go Remi! Go Remi" . . . smiling proudly."You have your Dads rythmn there."

"Move yourself 'bout Dads rythmn. You know it's me who taught her to dance." Sheresse dismissed Shokoyas boast, planting a kiss on her daughters forehead.

"Speaking of dancing there's a party in Maida Vale tonight ". . . Shokoya half heartedly suggested that Sheresse come with him.

"Don't bother with that Folabi you know how your Nigerian crowd stay. I love the food and all that but the girls them go on too bitchy and like they're so high and mighty and motor on in their Nigerian language . . ."

Shokoya raised his hand she didn't need to go on. He conceded the anti social traits of many a Nigerian girl. They had attended a Nigerian party before in St. Johns Wood two years ago. Sheresse brought her kid sister Dionne for moral support who caught the eye of one of the eligible bachelors attending. It turned out that one of the Nigerian girls at the party shared the same interest in this particular guy and noticed the overt moves Dionne had been making.

She rained abuse across the floor at her rival, it didn't need interpreting. Dionne went straight up in the girls face and challenged her. The threatened Nigerian girl made the first move and pushed Dionne away but ended up with her weave and pride scattered all over the floor as Dionne whipped her butt encouraged by her sister cheering her on. Shokoya took them home. Both girls laughed all the way while he contemplated how he would redeem his P.R . in the clique even though it wasn't Dionnes fault.

"Well it starts at around 9.00p.m. call me if you change your mind. How's Dionne anyway?" He said reaching into his pocket.

"She's fine." Sheresse replied with a tinge of guilt at Shokoya's good intentions.

"Here hold on to this." He slid her a brown envelope. " It doesn't have to be so formal you know . Why can't you move in with me?" He tried again to appeal to Shereese.

"Don't go there Folabi, it ain't happening . . . you know I like my independence. I have to have my own place and my own space." She left the envelope on the table knowing it contained money but looked at it to avert her eyes from Shokoyas pleading expression.

"O.K.when Mon Cheri, when?" Afolabi tried the nickname he'd given her six years before. He saw it didn't yield. Sheresse just sighed haunched her shoulders and opened her palms towards the ceiling.

"Daddy's got to go now, what do you want me to bring for you next time?"

"Erm erm a er " . . . Tamars indecision relayed she had almost every toy stuffed in her bed room.

"She's got enough toys already, you spoil her."

"O.K. come and give Daddy a hug." Tamar got down from her chair and stuffed the last of a hash brown into her mouth and gave Shokoya a greasy kiss.

"Daddy loves you." Shokoya reciprocated the affection. "You be a good girl OK"?

"I gotta go 'Folabi, I'll be late." Folabi picked up the envelope and put it in Sheresses hand he tried to look in her eyes while he held her hand but she looked down. "Look after yourself, you know I care about you."

"Thanks 'Folabi." She gave him a soft kiss on the lips he wanted to prolong it but let it slide. She turned and took her daughters hand as Tamar waved.

"Bye bye Daddy!" Tamars bottom lip quivered as she obediently followed her mother.

"Bye Remi."

He watched through the window as Sheresse secured her daughter in the baby seat next to her. He admired how good she looked. Still spunky and fit despite having a child and considered how relatively well the arranged marriage had worked out. He had known of guys who had married shire horses and white hiefers to legalise their stay with no question of a piece of the pussy thrown in for the bargain. Or those who had been shopped after paying out more than he had for the deal. While he had got lucky with a fine babe genuinely independently minded and had "his" child. But she wouldn't wear his ring or be right next to him as his woman.

"Maybe I should just count my blessings now." He thought to himself. But the truth was he was in too deep and falling deeper. Though he wouldn't admit it he loved his Sheresse and Tamar but he was sure she didn't feel the same.

He watched the metallic blue 306 pull away in the Saturday morning traffic and diminish as he reached for a newspaper on an adjacent table. He turned to the sports supplement and browsed over the football news. The bold print of a small headline in the corner caught his eye.

RANGERS WANT TO HAVE SOME FUN. He read the article about the Scottish clubs reported interest in his former school junior generated by his performances in the UEFA cup.

"The boy is setting himself up good. That's my guy. To know your way no be sin." He turned to the financial pages of the newspaper to check the share prices of his minor portfolio. He browsed over the share indexes till he found what he was looking for. TEN . . . up eight points. He had invested £700 in the summer of 1992 in shares in the retail outlet prices at the time were merely £1.59 at the time. They were now worth nearly four times that price.

"I say to know your way no be sin" he declared out loud.

"Oooh he's hit the bar!" Deoye thumbs worked frantically on the control pads of the Sony Playstation. John and he were playing FIFA 97 and John teased threatening to increase his 1-0 lead. John sensed victory as the game clock told one minute left. He hadn't beaten Deoye before and was looking forward to the prospect of doing so. Being in front with such little time left. He tried to kill time in possession, bad move. A software generated Arsenal midfielder pounced to make a tackle and release the ball to the Dennis Bergkamp replica. Deoye furrowed his brow further sensing his chance, now John worked frantically on the controls with his eyes fixed on the T.V. in his down stairs room.

The number ten figure released a cross to the far post and the John Hartson number nine replica headed goal bound.

"What a save!" John congratulated himself. No sooner said the Arsenal number eight figure drilled the ball into the goal.

"1-1!" Deoye heralded his equaliser with a punch of the air and a defiant scowl in Johns direction. The game played out a draw.

"Almost had you there Deoye, almost had you."

"True, but I wasn't concentrating properly." His mind had been on going out with Funmi since the morning . The whole day seemed to drag by as a prelude to the evening's main event.

"Ahh rubbish! I was all over you admit it."

"Whatever John. What's the time?"

"It's only 6.30 p.m. Lets have another game?"

"Can't do John I gotta be out by 7.30 sorry. Besides aren't you watching Anaconda with Karen."

"Yeah but it won't take me that long to get ready. Come on I can taste it I'll whip you this time." John insisted.

"Whip me? Whip me? I knew you were like that all along. You had to mention whips didn't you it's all coming out now . Niggers been struggling since I got off the boat now Massa Fuller gon' whip my ass." Deoye teased in a mock southern states accent, as he walked out of Johns room and up the stairs. "Go and get ready to watch the big snake John . I've seen it already."

"What was it like?"

"Big brown and very alive. You would be totally unfamiliar with such. Karen might like it though." Deoye elevated the teasing with a little innuendo.

"I don't know about that, but that Jennifer Lopez . . . phfwooagh!" John commented.

"That's what I'm talkin' about?" Deoye agreed."Oh sorry Vicky I thought you were out."

Vicky emerged from her bedroom her face flushed white and pale, her hair scattered and wispy looking. She was holding her stomach. All her symptoms told that she was suffering from her monthly girly problems. "You look like you need to go there more than me." Vicky murmured something about being woken by boys talk and closed the bathroom door behind her. Deoye squeezed into his bedroom and looked at the clothes he had selected to wear on the bed. "Yeah this'll do the job."

An Italian cotton / linen mix royal blue four button single breasted casual suit and a light blue chambray shirt looked crisp. He considered a choice of shoes. A black pair of flat leather square toed Nordstorm slip ons or the brown loafers he had worn to the interview at TEN. He hated wearing leather soles unless he was driving but he was yet to wear the shoes his cousin Henry had sent from New York for Xmas the occasion hadn't arisen. He pulled the shoe box out from under the bed and stroked the soft ebony calf leather, triggering thoughts of all the honeys that would be up in the joint.

He hadn't had some since that new year party that Femi threw. The party had a ratio of 3:2 girls to guys. Like all Femis party's it was a meat market, he couldn't fail to score. He picked up on a sexy clad sister that was up in his face all night.

In Nkechis eyes Deoye couldn't do no wrong, he hadn't even began his nought to sixty on the pretty petite Igbo girl. Though he was down for whatever after half a bottle of Malibu, she reached up and whispered in his ear her plans for the night. And while Deoye was figuring out if it was the alcohol or Nkechi talking she led him out of the party drove him to her flat in Finchley where they went head to head for the rest of the night and most of the morning.

They were mutually impressed with each others bed room repertoire though Deoye was half stoned. He had reservations about calling Nkechi up again thinking she was too independent and a man eating nympho though she still called him from time to time.

Deoye heard the bathroom door open, stripped naked and grabbed his bath robe. He entered the bathroom with a hard on precipitated from his sexual reminiscing and his lustful thoughts of Nkechi. Thirty five minutes later after a hot shower he was still hard as he came out of the steamy bathroom. Still dripping he didn't bother completely drying himself as he looked for a fresh pair Joe Boxers, which again his cousin Henry sent regularly from stateside. He prefered these to the clinging jersey Calvin Klien's or Tommy Hilfiger types that didn't give a nigga room down there.

He sprayed his body liberally with Anteaus, his trade mark cologne, daxed his fade then brushed his full eye brows. He hung his robe and dressed meticulously. He toyed with the idea of tucking in his shirt but remembered Funmis instructions,smart but casual.

Satisfied that the rounded bottom of the shirt looked smart enough against the soft blue fabric of his trousers. He pulled on a pair of blue burlingtons, slipped on the loafers and stood up looking in the mirror admiring how the trousers dropped on the shoes. He afforded himself a smile whilst checking out his reflection. He pulled on his jacket to complete the outfit. "Yeah" he thought all blue with black highlights his ring and ear stud spade punctuated the whole look black and blue Deoye hoped his pride or ego wouldn't be bruised before the night was through. He looked out of the window it was raining lightly.

"I'm gonna have to take a cab to Funmi's." Eating at his limited budget some more.

"Looking smart " John commented coming down the stairs wearing jeans while buttoning a Ben Sherman shirt.

"Thanks John. Like I said I'm going out tonight."

"Yeah I heard you're going near Brent Street you want a lift?"

"No thanks John." John was already running late and Deoye didn't want any excuses for not being in time. He went to the sitting room and put on the text to check on the scores from the NBA. As Victoria came into the sitting room. "How're you feeling?"

She wasn't comfortable with the ease with which Deoye was able to talk about girly problems with apparent genuine concern.

"I'm all right thanks." She replied passing him and going into kitchen.

"You smell nice where you going tonight?"

"I'm hooking up with a friend we are going to a party in Maida Vale." Deoye surveyed the basketball scores as they flashed up. The Bulls won again no surprise.

"Do you want a coffee Deoye?"

"No thanks Vicky. No thanks."

Amane's door bell rang.

"Pizzas here" Priti shouted grabbing her purse and heading for the door. She had been busy on her PC writing her disitation to the jazzy sound of Eryka.

"That was quick." Amane said looking at the clock. It was 7.48. It hadn't been five minutes since she ordered the pizza. Too concerned with her hunger to take a peep through the spy hole, Priti opened the door with her head down picking notes and change out of her purse. When she looked up she was surprised. She slowly looked up, no bikers boots, no leathers, no crash helmet. She looked at the smart black guy disappointed.

"Where's the pizza?"

"Excuse me?" Deoye wasn't sure he had heard correctly. "I'm looking for a Miss Funmi Somefun."

"Oh I'm sorry." Priti covered her mouth and moved to one side inviting Deoye in.

"You must be Funmis cousin Deoye right?" Deoye ignored Priti's misappropriation of his and Funmi's relationship.

"Another girl killing those hipsters" he thought taking in Priti's petite figure. Priti offered her hand.

"Hi I'm Priti."

"You certainly are but isn't that stating the obvious, if not being vain?" Deoye offered a sample of his charm.

"Ah hah! Corney if not charming." Priti smiled. "Funmis in the bath at the moment I'll give her a shout , take a seat."

"How much do I owe you Polly?" Amane stepped out of her room. Deoye pivoted his head to the source of the voice. The long jersey dress Amani wore emphasised her elongated hour glass shape. She wasn't wearing a bra her nipples were visibly protruding through the cotton fabric, which after Deoye had appreciated her hips, is where he momentarily brought his eyes to focus before her face. Amane noticed the earring spade stud, the profile, the furrowed brow.

"You're Funmi's cousin!?"

Deoye smiled. " I don't mean to be corny . . . again," he glanced at Priti, "but haven't we met before?

I can't quite remember the time or the place."

Amane was recomposed and she also glanced at Priti who by now had sensed something was up. She played dumb.

" Maybe we have met before. My name's Amane, does that ring any bells?"

"No but ". . . .

"And you're Funmis cousin Deoye right?" Amane continued at a pace even Priti was impressed with. "Can I get you something to drink? Coke, Orange juice, Ribena . . . BLACKBERRY JUICE maybe hmm?"

Just before the exaggerated pronunciation of the beverage it all clicked. Deoye bit his bottom lip and squinted as he recollected his embarrassing first encounter with Amane. She put her head side ways and waited for his verbal response as she crossed her arms over her chest and leaned against the door post.

"Agghh you got me." Deoye's mind clicked as Funmi entered.

"Glad to see you guys are getting acquainted." Funmi stepped out of her room looking sexily dressed and classy in a coffee coloured evening dress with thin shoulder straps and a long central leg revealing split. Her jaw bone and dimples accentuated by subtly applied make up.

"You changed your mind I see, looking good all the same." Priti approved. Amane nodded in agreement.

"Yes we have met before though we didn't get as far as exchanging names."

"Black coffee, no sugar, no cream, that's the kind of girl I like down with my team." Deoye sang the line to distract Amane from spilling the beans. "Come and gi' me some love, long time no see." Funmi and Deoye embraced. Funmi broke off.

"This is my crazy cousin Deoye, affectionately called D. Deoye meet my landlady and friend Amane and friend and confidant Priti."

"We got that far Funmi. Sorry I thought he was the pizza boy, I'm starving. Uni work always makes me stuff myself sorry Deoye." Priti apologised as she looked at her watch.

"Well I guess you don't do that much studying cos your figure doesn't suggest so." Deoye commented as the door bell rang .

Priti smiled "We like this guy Funny. Yep we like this guy." She went to answer the door.

"That'll be the pizza, do you want some before you go Funmi?"

"No thanks Amane. Unlike Polly I have to work at keeping the weight down you know how it is." Funmi shook her head at Deoye's flirting but fished for parallel compliments.

"And my eyes now behold the positive results of your hard work." She received one

"Thank you Deoye."

"You're welcome." He looked at Amane once more desperate to keep the flow away from any recollection of their first encounter. She spared him the embarrassment." Pizza for you, or just the drink Deoye hmm?" She raised that eye brow again teasingly.

"Er just the drink thanks, orange juice."

"One Bla . . . orange juice coming up." Amane turned and headed for the kitchen, Priti soon joined her with a medium Pizza and a tub of Hagen Dazs.

"Don't tell me that's the guy on the train?" She asked in a forceful whisper.

"Uh-huh that's him Polly."

"Stop it! Does Funmi know?"

"I've not had the chance to tell her, do you think I should?"

"Yeah! And judging by the way he's dressed tonight he certainly doesn't need to be signing on. You know how she feels about Nigerians giving her country a bad name. He comes in here looking all smooth while he's running benefit fraud. Let Funmi know Empress, let her speak to him cos they go way back."

Priti spoke frankly and concerned as she cut the pizza into segments and looked in the fridge for a salad. Amane finished pouring the drink, something told her to hold back.

"I hear you Priti but I wont say anything tonight, not as they're about to go out. Besides he might just mention it himself. "

Priti prepared two plates of pasta salad as she watched Deoye and Funmi laughing and joking with each other in the sitting room. "It's a shame though, he's kinda cute."

"Now, now that's tabu Polly." Amane reminded her as she stepped out of the kitchen with two glasses.

"Hmm that looks good and that drink looks refreshing too." Deoye offered another corney compliment with a pleading look into Amane's eyes. She gave him a reassuring smile.

"Is he always like this Funmi?" she handed him the drink.

"Well he usually behaves himself when we're out but Deoye does say what he means and means what he says, which while sometimes can be flattering, also gets him into trouble too."

"I tell it like it is that's all." Deoye thanked Amane and took a sip of his drink whilst comparing the three fine girls as Priti came out of the kitchen and set a tray of food on the table.

" I'm all for speaking what's on my mind too Deoye. Are you sure you don't want something before you go?" Deoye looked at the three of them and considered a smutty reply but dismissed it as he lowered his glass.

"No I'm O.K. Thanks for offering though."

"Let me get my keys and we'll be off. I'm not into this African time thing."

"Can I drive please? Oh please, oh please, oh please? Deoye said with a child like lisp."

Funmi came out of her room, dangling her keys in her hand while putting on a tan crochet cardigan.

"Catch!" Deoye caught the keys left handed and waved with his right.

"I'll see you again some time. Thanks for the drink the next one is on me."

"Yeah make mine a blackberry juice." Priti gave Amane a disapproving look.

Funmi showed no signs that she had caught on to the joke. She picked up a small clutch bag.

"O.K. How do I look?" She asked the routine question before she went out.

Priti gave her the thumbs up as she put an anchovie into her mouth.

"Have some fun, you hear?"

"Some fun is my last name." Funmi looped her arm in Deoye's who was already waiting with the door ajar and they waved and shut the door behind them.

Eryka Badu played on for a good twenty minutes uninterrupted. Neither girl spoke till Priti broke the silence. "So would you have him Empress?"

"Priti!" Amane was embarrassed Priti had read her mind it was all over her face.

"Come on don't play coy with me. Would you?" Priti persisted.

Amane took a scoop of the Baileys/Hagen Dazs ice cream and looked down.

"Yeah I'd go out with him O.K!" She took another scoop and licked the spoon provocatively with exaggerated slowness. "Mmmmm" she was engrossed in her thoughts, they tasted good. "Um-hum I would go out with him."